GERMANY

Gerhart H. Seger

Gerhart H. Seger is a well-known author, newspaper correspondent, and lecturer. He was born in Germany and was a member of the German Reichstag (national legislature) from 1930 to 1933. He came to the United States in 1934 and is now a naturalized American citizen. Mr. Seger has made several recent trips to the country of his birth and writes about Germany from a background of years of study and travel.

LIBRARY OF CONGRESS CATALOG CARD NUMBER: 66-16535

EDITORS AND ADVISORS

EUROPE

NORWAY	**FRANCE**
SWEDEN	**SWITZERLAND**
THE BRITISH ISLES	**AUSTRIA**
THE NETHERLANDS	**ITALY**
GERMANY	**SPAIN**

SOVIET UNION

ASIA, AFRICA, AUSTRALIA

CHINA	**INDIA**
SOUTHEAST ASIA	**AFRICA**
JAPAN	**AUSTRALIA**

GERMANY

Gerhart H. Seger

THE FIDELER COMPANY

GRAND RAPIDS   TORONTO

CONTENTS

Maps and Special Studies

EDITORIAL AND MAP ACKNOWLEDGMENTS

Grateful acknowledgment is made to Scott, Foresman and Company for the pronunciation system used in this book, which is taken from the *Thorndike-Barnhart Dictionary Series*.

Grateful acknowledgment is made to the following for permission to use cartographic data in this book: McGraw-Hill Book Company: Pages 132 and 133; Nystrom Raised Relief Map Company, Chicago, Illinois 60618: Page 175; Panoramic Studios: Pages 8 and 9; United States Department of Commerce, Bureau of Census: Adapted map on page 174.

PICTURE ACKNOWLEDGMENTS

Grateful acknowledgment is made to the following for permission to use the illustrations found in this book: Aero-Photo — München-Gladbach, Germany: Page 92 by Schwarzer; Almasy — Paris, France: Pages 24 and 106; Barnaby's Picture Library — London, England: Page 142; Bavaria-Verlag — Munich, Germany: Pages 22, 29, 97, 103, and 164; Beerhorst: Page 39; Bettmann Archive: Pages 36, 47, 51, 55, and 57 (upper); Black Star: Pages 54, 59, 66, 68, 78 (lower), and 159; page 35 (upper) by Ewen; pages 35 (right) and 84 by Koenig; and page 145 by Lackenbach; Brown Brothers: Page 50; Bundesbildstelle — Bonn, Germany: Pages 15, 73, 123, 134 (upper), 137, 152, and 158; Cash — London, England: Page 33; Collins: Page 42; Devaney: Page 93; Dale DeWitt: Page 112; Eastfoto: Pages 35 (lower left), 61, 63 (right), 88, 89, 91 (lower), 100, 127, 144, 154, 167, and 168; European Community Information Service: Page 14 (lower); European Picture Service: Pages 83 and 166; R. E. Fideler: Pages 113, 119, and 122 (prints by Malloy); French Government Tourist Office: Page 12 (upper); Galloway: Page 139; German Information Center: Pages 16, 75, and 77; German Tourist Information Office: Pages 3, 129 (upper), and 156; Hehmke Winterer — Düsseldorf, Germany: Page 131 (lower); Historical Pictures Service: Page 49; Historisches Bildarchiv — Bad Berneck, Germany: Pages 37, 40, and 44; Keystone Press: Page 157; Lufthansa German Airlines: Page 124; Magnum Photos, Inc.: Page 141; Malloy: Page 169; Mangold — Bonn, Germany: Pages 82 and 91 (upper); Netherlands Information Service: Page 12 (lower); Photo Researchers, Inc.: Pages 143 by Angermayer and 163 by Henle; Pictorial Parade, Inc.: Pages 57 (lower), 63 (left), 65, 67, 76, 78 (upper), 81, 87, and 96; Pix, Inc.: Pages 70, 108 (lower), and 116; Poppel — Stockholm, Sweden: Page 128; Radio Free Europe: Page 126; Rudolphi — Braunlage/Harz, Germany: Page 23; Saebens Worpswede — Bremen, Germany: Pages 21, 27 (lower), 105, 111, 115, 118, 131 (upper), 146, and 151; Schneiders — Lindau-Schachen, Germany: Pages 108 (upper), 134 (lower), 150, and 165; Sovfoto: Page 71 by Haldei; Three Lions, Inc.: Pages 60, 130, and 135; Traubenkraut — Ettringen-Eifel, Germany: Page 110; Wide World Photos: Page 14 (upper); Wolff and Tritschler — Frankfurt am Main, Germany: Pages 17, 19, 26, 27 (upper), 94, 104, 107, 129 (lower), and 161; Zentralbild — Berlin, Germany: Pages 79, 148, 149, 155 (both), and 160.

TO THE STUDENT

Why the social studies are important to you. During the next few years, you will make an important choice. You will choose whether or not you will direct your own life. Many people are never aware of making this choice. They drift through life, never really trying to understand what is going on around them or why things turn out the way they do. Without knowing it, these people have chosen not to direct their own lives. As a result, they miss many enriching experiences. Other people make a serious effort to choose a way of life that will bring them satisfaction. The chances are that you will have a more challenging life if you decide to live by choice instead of by chance.

You will need three types of knowledge to live successfully by choice. Living by choice will demand a great deal from you. You will have to keep growing in three different types of learnings — understandings, attitudes, and skills. As the chart below shows, the type of learning we call understandings includes the kinds of information you need in order to understand yourself, your country, and your world. The type of learning we call attitudes deals with the way you feel toward yourself and your world. The third type of learning includes the different kinds of skills you need to use in gaining understandings and developing constructive attitudes. Among these skills are knowing how to locate, evaluate, and organize information, how to read with understanding, and how to work effectively with others.

The social studies can help you grow in the three types of learnings. Your social studies class is one of the best places in which you can explore the three types of learnings. Here you can obtain much of the information you need for understanding yourself and your world. You can practice many important skills. Through many experiences, you can begin to evaluate what in life is worthwhile to you.

The problem-solving method will help you achieve success in social studies. Since the social studies are of such great importance, you want to use the best possible study method. Of course, you could just read a textbook and memorize answers for a test. If you did so, however, you would forget much of the information soon after the test was over. Your attitudes would not develop, and you would not have the opportunity to use many important skills. We suggest that you use a better way of studying. This is the problem-solving method. To use this method in learning about Germany, you will need to follow these steps:

1. Do some general background reading about Germany, or about a particular aspect of Germany that you want to explore.

2. Choose an important, interesting problem that you would like to solve about Germany. Write it down so that

Three Types of Learnings

Understandings	Attitudes	Skills
A. Facts	A. Values*	A. Obtaining knowledge
B. Concepts*	B. Appreciations*	B. Handling knowledge
C. Generalizations*	C. Ideals	C. Working with people

*See glossary

you will have clearly in mind what it is you want to find out. (Note the sample problems on this page.) If there are small problems that need to be solved in order to solve your big problem, list them, too.

3. Consider all possible solutions to your problem and list the ones that seem most likely to be true. These possible solutions are called "educated guesses," or hypotheses. You will try to solve your problem by proving that these hypotheses are true or false. Some will be partly true and partly false.

4. Find out which hypotheses are correct or partly correct by doing research. List the important information that is related to your hypotheses. If the information in different sources conflicts, check further and try to decide which information is correct.

5. Summarize what you have learned. Have you proved or disproved your hypotheses? What new facts have you learned? Do you need to do further research?

You may want to write a report about the problem and the solution or solutions that you believe to be correct. To help other people share the ideas that you have come to understand, you may decide to illustrate your research project with maps, pictures, or your own drawings. You will find helpful suggestions for writing a good report on pages 181 and 182.

You can use the problem-solving method throughout your life. In addition to helping you to achieve success in the social studies, the problem-solving method can help you in another way. By using it, you will learn a way of dealing with problems that will be valuable to you throughout your life. Many successful scientists, businessmen, and government leaders use this method to solve problems.

When you have a problem to solve, you need all the information you can find to reach a correct solution. This Depth-Study Textbook was written especially for students who are using the problem-solving method. It contains four main sources of information: text, pictures, maps, and glossary items. To locate the specific information you want, you may use the Table of Contents and the Index. The suggestions on pages 178-180 will help you to locate and evaluate other sources of information.

Sample problems to solve. You may wish to solve these problems as you study about Germany.

1. **Germany has been divided for more than twenty years, and there seems to be little chance of reuniting the country in the near future. What has caused this situation?** In forming hypotheses, you will want to consider the following:

   a. Germany's history

   b. how valuable East and West Germany have been to their respective allies in the Cold War

   c. the present attitude that the Communist and non-Communist nations have toward each other

2. **The longer Germany remains divided, the harder it will be for East and West Germany to work together as parts of the same country if they are reunited. Why is this so?**

   a. How would the difference in the way factories and farms are run in East and West Germany make it difficult for the two parts of the country to work together if they are reunited?

   b. How would differences in the educational systems of East and West Germany make great adjustments necessary in a reunited Germany?

North Pole

ASIA

PACIFIC OCEAN

NORTH AMERICA

Across the North Pole from North America is Eurasia, the largest single area of land in the world. The eastern part of this landmass is Asia, and the western part is Europe.

Divided Germany in Europe

Where is Germany? If you could see the earth from space, it would look much like the globes pictured on these two pages. Most of the earth's surface is covered with water. Lying like huge islands in the water are several large masses of land. The largest of these is Eurasia, which is located across the North Pole from North America.

As the maps on pages 9, 10, and 11 show, Eurasia is crossed by many man-made boundaries. One boundary divides Eurasia into two continents, Europe and Asia. Other boundaries divide these

North · Pole

EUROPE

ASIA

AFRICA

INDIAN OCEAN

Europe is one of the world's smallest continents. About the same size as the United States, it is divided into many countries. Divided Germany is located in the heart of Europe.

two continents into countries. Among the countries in the heart of Europe is Germany.

A man-made boundary divides Germany into two parts, East Germany and West Germany. How did this division take place, and what significance does it have? To answer these questions, you will need to go beyond the man-made borders of Germany and look

briefly at the continent of which this divided country is a part.

Europe — a small continent of many countries. Europe is one of the smallest continents on the globe. It is about the same size as the United States. The largest country in Europe is the Soviet Union. It occupies about half the continent and extends on across the entire northern part of Asia. Most of Europe's

EUROPE

Scale of Miles

0 50 100   200   300   400

⊗ National Capitals   ● Other Cities

Shading from green through yellow, brown, and red indicates increase in altitude. Figures show approximate altitude in feet for corresponding color.

10,000 ft.

5,000 ft.

2,000 ft.

1,000 ft.

500 ft.

COPYRIGHT BY RAND MC NALLY & CO. MADE IN U.S.A.

ARCTIC CIRCLE

ICELAND

Reykjavik ⊗

NORWEGIAN SEA

NORWAY

SWEDEN

GULF OF

Faeroe Islands

Shetland Islands

Bergen ●

Oslo ⊗

Stockholm ⊗

Göteborg ●

BALTIC

Glasgow ●

Edinburgh ●

Belfast ●

Dublin ⊗

IRELAND

NORTH SEA

DENMARK

Copenhagen ⊗

Liverpool ●

UNITED KINGDOM

London ⊗

Hamburg ●

Elbe

Berlin ⊗

NETHERLANDS

Amsterdam ⊗

Essen ●

Cologne ●

Rhine

Oder River

Vistula River

POLA

GERMANY

ATLANTIC OCEAN

ENGLISH CHANNEL

Antwerp ●

BELGIUM

Brussels ⊗

Bonn ●

LUX.

Prague ⊗

CZECHOSLOVA

Nantes ●

Paris ⊗

Seine River

Loire

Danube

River

Munich ●

Vienna ⊗

Budapest ⊗

HUNGA

Bay of Biscay

Bordeaux ●

FRANCE

Lyon ●

SWITZERLAND

Bern ⊗

ALPS

AUSTRIA

Drava River

YUGOSLA

Rhône River

Milan ●

Venice ●

Bilbao ●

PYRENEES

Garonne River

Po River

Genoa ●

Florence ●

I

T

A

L

Y

APENNINES

ADRIATIC SEA

Marseille ●

PORTUGAL

SPAIN

Lisbon ⊗

Madrid ⊗

Barcelona ●

CORSICA

Rome ⊗

Córdoba ●

Balearic Islands

Naples ●

Tirane ⊗

Seville ●

Cartagena ●

SARDINIA

M

E

D

I

T

E

R

R

A

N

STRAIT OF GIBRALTAR

Tangier ●

Algiers ⊗

SICILY

IONIAN SEA

Casablanca ●

Rabat ⊗

Tunis ⊗

MALTA

A

F

R

I

C

A

ATLAS MOUNTAINS

Tripoli ●

West Longitude   0°   East Longitude

20° 30° 40° 50° 60° 70° 60°

ARCTIC CIRCLE

•Murmansk

Ob River

Irtysh River

FINLAND
BOTHNIA

WHITE
SEA

•Arkhangelsk

N. Dvina River

URAL MOUNTAINS

•Omsk

Sverdlovsk• •Chelyabinsk

Helsinki

•Leningrad

Volga Gorkiy River
•Kazan

50°

SEA

Riga

MOSCOW ⊕

•Kuybyshev

S O V I E T

Minsk

U N I O N

Ural River

ARAL
SEA

Warsaw
⊕

ND

Kiev•
Dnepr River

Don River

Kharkov•

Volgograd•

Volga River

•Astrakhan

C

A

S

I

A

KIA
CARPATHIANS

U K R A I N E

Dnestr River

Rostov•

Odessa•

CAUCASUS MOUNTAINS

P

I

RY
ROMANIA

CRIMEA

SEA OF
AZOV

Mt.
Elbrus

Baku•

A

N

40°

Belgrade• Bucharest•
Moravа River
Danube River

Sevastopol•

B L A C K   S E A

Batumi•

S

E

A

•Tabriz

•Tehran
⊕

VIA

BULGARIA
Sofia ⊕

Istanbul•
BOSPORUS

ANATOLIAN PLATEAU Mt.
Ararat

ALBANIA

DARDANELLES

Ankara
⊕

T U R K E Y

I

R

A

N

Mt. +
Olympus

AEGEAN

ASIA   MINOR

Tigris

•Esfahan

GREECE
Athens ⊕

SEA

Izmir•

Aleppo•

S Y R I A

Euphrates River

Baghdad•
⊕

•North Latitude

30°

Rhodes

CYPRUS

I R A Q

•Abadan

River

Crete

LEBANON
Beirut• ⊕ •Damascus

Basra•

KUWAIT

E A N   S E A

ISRAEL
Tel Aviv•

Amman•
⊕

PERSIAN GULF

20° 30°

Jerusalem• ⊕ JORDAN

40° 50°

other countries can be compared in size to individual states in the United States. France, for example, is a little smaller than Texas, and Belgium is about the size of Maryland.

One of the world's most productive continents. Europe is one of the most productive continents in the world. Its factories produce a larger amount of manufactured goods than the factories of any other continent except North America. Together, the countries of Europe carry on more trade than the combined countries of any other continent.

There are several reasons why Europe is so productive. First, it has many of the natural resources needed for farming and manufacturing. Second, it has a long coastline with many harbors where trading ships can load and unload goods. Its central location in relation to Asia, Africa, and the Americas is also

A steel plant in France. Europe produces a larger amount of manufactured goods than any other continent except North America.

favorable for trade. As a result, raw materials and other goods that Europe does not produce can be shipped in from other continents without great difficulty.

Geography alone did not cause Europe's countries to become so productive, however. The attitudes and skills of Europe's people also were important. These people have shown great energy and inventiveness in developing their continent's resources and advantages for trade.

A continent that has helped to shape the course of history. The small, productive continent of Europe has played an important part in world affairs. It is the birthplace of Western civilization. Europeans helped to spread Western ideas and customs to other parts of the world by leaving their countries and settling in the Americas and other distant lands.

The port of Rotterdam. The combined countries of Europe carry on more trade than the combined countries of any other continent.

Europe has influenced history in another way. During most of the past two and one-half centuries, the leading countries of the world were located in Europe. These countries were so powerful that they were able to influence a large part of the world. They took over vast areas in Asia and Africa and established large empires. Frequently, they fought with each other for territory and power. Two conflicts between European nations spread until they involved almost every part of the world. These were World War I and World War II. As Chapter 4 shows, the two world wars brought great destruction to Europe.

A divided continent. Since World War II another conflict called the Cold War has divided the countries of Europe into two main groups. This conflict is a result of the Soviet Union's determination to bring the world under communism and the equal determination of democratic nations to prevent it from doing so. The Soviet army occupied much of eastern Europe during and after World War II. It helped to establish Communist governments in the east European countries under its occupation.

The countries of western Europe needed help to stop the spread of communism, for they were still suffering from the damages of World War II. They received help from the United States. The United States granted vast amounts of aid to these nations to use in repairing the damages caused by the war. In addition, the United States and Canada joined with several European nations in an anti-Communist military alliance called the North Atlantic Treaty Organization, or NATO. These and other measures successfully stopped the spread of communism in Europe. They did not, however, free the countries in the eastern part of the continent that were already under Communist control. Today, these eastern European nations form a separate group that is developing along very different lines from the rest of Europe. The imaginary dividing

THE SPREAD OF COMMUNISM IN EURASIA

 Communist

Non-Communist

The announced goal of Communists everywhere is to bring the world under communism. The first country in which Communists gained power was Russia, where a Communist government was established in 1917. Since that time, the Communists have made great strides toward their goal of world domination. Today, about two thirds of Eurasia is under Communist rule, and a Communist beachhead in the Americas has been established in Cuba.

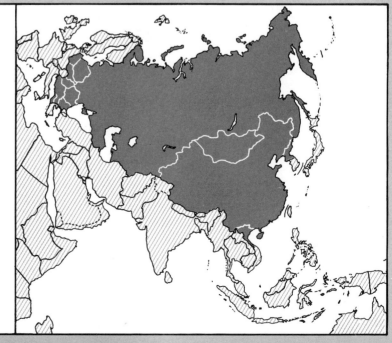

A NATO meeting in Paris. The United States helped to form NATO after World War II to stop the spread of communism.

Germany has played an important part in the development of Europe. Germany has helped to shape much of what has happened in Europe through the years. Some of Germany's influence has been good. For example, German writers, composers, scientists, and inventors have contributed much to the art and technology* of Europe. All of Germany's influence has not been good, however. The actions and ambitions of people in Germany have helped to bring about much of the warfare Europe has suffered. Germany's desire for power and land was one of the main causes of World War I and World War II.

Germany became a divided country after World War II. Events in other parts of Europe have helped to shape Germany's history. One of the goals of the Soviet Union after World War II was to bring Germany under Communist control. The Soviets succeeded in establishing a Communist government in the

*See glossary

A meeting of European Community leaders. Several countries in western Europe are working together through cooperative associations.

line between the Communist and non-Communist parts of Europe is called the Iron Curtain.

The nations of western Europe may be moving toward unity. In the part of Europe outside the Iron Curtain, an important change has been taking place. A number of nations here have come to realize that they are handicapped by their small size. To overcome this handicap, they have begun to cooperate among themselves to form larger groups, or associations. Outstanding among these cooperative groups is the European Community, which is discussed on page 98. The spirit of cooperation in western Europe, together with the help this area received from the United States, has made it possible for most of the countries here to become more prosperous than ever before in their history.

The Berlin Philharmonic Orchestra. Germany has contributed much to the art and technology* of Europe. However, Germany's desire for power has caused much suffering and destruction.

eastern part of Germany, which was occupied by Soviet soldiers. However, Britain, France, and the United States prevented this from happening in the western part of Germany. Today, Germany is divided into two main parts, East Germany and West Germany. East Germany has a Communist government and has close ties with other Communist countries behind the Iron Curtain. West Germany has a democratic government and is an important member of NATO and the European Community.

The two major divisions of Germany, East and West Germany, are so independent of each other that they are considered to be separate countries. However, the name "Germany" is still used by many people. In this book, it will be used when the combined geographical area of East and West Germany is discussed. It will also be used to refer to the country of Germany before it was divided and to the reunited country that many Germans hope one day to see again.

The future of divided Germany. Although many Germans would like to see Germany reunited, it does not seem likely that this will happen in the near future. The border between East and

West Germany is part of the boundary between the Communist and non-Communist parts of Europe. Neither side in the Cold War is willing to give up its part of Germany in order for the country to be reunited.

The longer that the East and West Germans remain separated, the harder it will be for them to work together as citizens of one country if they are ever reunited. The following chapters show why. Education and government are very different in the two parts of Germany. The way farms and factories are run in West Germany differs from the way they are run in East Germany. As the years pass, the people in each part of this divided country are becoming more accustomed to the way things are done in their part of Germany. The Germans still have much in common, however. If the country is reunited, it will be interesting to see whether or not the ways in which they are alike are important enough to overcome the ways in which they are different.

The Berlin Wall was built by the Communists in 1961 to prevent people in East Germany from escaping to West Germany. It does not seem likely that Germany will be reunited in the near future.

Germany is a land of plains, rolling hills, wide rivers, and snow-covered mountain peaks. The Germans have made good use of their beautiful land.

Part 1

Land and Climate

NORTH SEA

BALTIC SEA

DENMARK

NETHERLANDS

POLAND

⊙ Hamburg

● Bremen

Elbe R.

Oder R.

Berlin ⊙

Weser R.

Ems R.

● Hanover

East Germany

HARZ MOUNTAINS

Duisburg ●   ● Dortmund

Essen ●

● Düsseldorf

Ruhr R.

● Leipzig

Cologne ●

BELGIUM

Bonn ★

Rhine R.

ORE MOUNTAINS

Neisse R.

LUX.

● Frankfurt am Main

Main R.

CZECHOSLOVAKIA

Elbe R.

West   Germany

BOHEMIAN FOREST

Stuttgart ○

Danube R.

FRANCE

BLACK FOREST

Rhine R.

Danube R.

Munich ⊙

BAVARIAN ALPS

SWITZERLAND

AUSTRIA

GERMANY

Elevation in Feet

Sea Level to 500
500 to 1,000
1,000 to 2,000
2,000 to 5,000
5,000 and Over

Cities

● 500,000 to 1,000,000
⊙ 1,000,000 and Over
★ Capitals

Scale of Miles

0   25   50   75

18

ITALY

Rhine Valley farmlands. Germany, which is politically divided into East and West Germany, is located in the heart of Europe. It is a little more than half the size of Texas.

1 Land

A Study Guide

Thoughts To Help You

Germany has a variety of land features. These include lowlands, rolling hills, wide rivers, and snow-covered mountain peaks. As you read this chapter, look for answers to the following questions:

1. How does the land differ from north to south?
2. Why is the highland region almost as densely populated as the lowland?

Terms To Understand

You need to know the following terms in order to read this chapter with understanding. Look up terms you do not know in the glossary of this book, a dictionary, or an encyclopedia.

dike
elevation
highland
lowland

loess
moor
plateau
sea level

Germany is located in the heart of Europe. It has an area of 137,743 square miles, which makes it a little more than half the size of Texas. West Germany occupies about seven tenths of this area. The rest is occupied by East Germany.

The land of Germany differs considerably from north to south. A great lowland stretches across the northern part. In central and southern Germany there are plateaus, rolling hills, and mountain ranges.

Land Regions

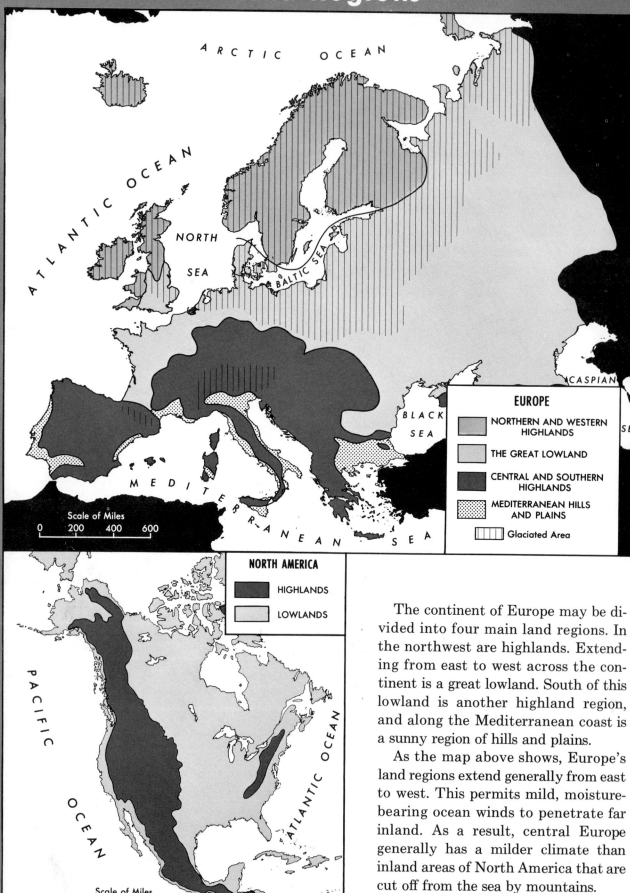

The continent of Europe may be divided into four main land regions. In the northwest are highlands. Extending from east to west across the continent is a great lowland. South of this lowland is another highland region, and along the Mediterranean coast is a sunny region of hills and plains.

As the map above shows, Europe's land regions extend generally from east to west. This permits mild, moisture-bearing ocean winds to penetrate far inland. As a result, central Europe generally has a milder climate than inland areas of North America that are cut off from the sea by mountains.

Northern Germany. The lowland that covers northern Germany is part of a larger lowland that extends through Europe from southern France to the Ural Mountains. (Compare map on opposite page with map on pages 10 and 11.) Most of the land in Germany's northern lowland region is less than five hundred feet above sea level. Scattered throughout this region are lakes, moors, and marshes. Much marshland has been made suitable for grass to grow and is now pastureland. In the northwestern corner of the lowland region, some of the land has been reclaimed from the North Sea and is protected by dikes.

The southern part of the lowland, which merges with the highlands to the south, is gently rolling.

The soil differs from place to place in the lowland of northern Germany. Along the southern edge of this lowland region are areas of very fertile soil called loess.* Some of Germany's best farmlands are located here. The northern part of the lowland has much poorer soil. With the help of fertilizers, however, German farmers in the north are able to obtain abundant harvests of such crops as rye, oats, and potatoes.

Many rivers flow across the lowland. Among the most important are the

*See glossary

Dikes in the coastal areas of northwestern Germany protect land that has been reclaimed from the sea. Here, and in the other parts of northern Germany, the land is generally low.

The Ruhr industrial area is located in the southwestern part of the lowland region that covers northern Germany. There are rich deposits of high-quality coal in the southern part of the lowland. Areas of very fertile soil are found here, also.

Rhine, the Elbe, and the Weser. These rivers flow from the highlands into the North Sea.

Many large cities and industrial areas are located in the lowland. The Ruhr industrial area, with its busy cities and giant industries, lies in the southwestern part of the lowland. Berlin, Germany's largest city, lies in the eastern part. Hamburg and Bremen, two important ports of Germany, are located near the North Sea coast.

Central and southern Germany. The highlands of central and southern Germany are part of a larger highland region that extends through central and southern Europe. Compared to other highland areas of the world, the highlands of central and southern Germany are relatively low. Much of the land is less than five thousand feet above sea level. With the exception of the Bavarian Alps, the mountain ranges here are old and rounded.

In central Germany, the lowland merges with highlands. The central and southern parts of Germany are located in Europe's central and southern highland region. Most of the land in this part of Germany consists of hills, plateaus, and mountains. 23

In the Bavarian Alps of southern Germany are snow-covered peaks that rise as high as nine thousand feet above sea level. Most of the mountains in Germany, however, are low and rounded.

Much of central Germany consists of plateaus and rolling hills. However, there are also several mountain ranges here. Two of these are the Harz Mountains, located on the northern border of the highland region, and the Ore Mountains, located on the southern border of East Germany.

A large plateau covers part of southern Germany. This plateau, with its scattered lakes, rolling hills, and river valleys, rises gradually to the foot of the Bavarian Alps.

The Bavarian Alps have snow-covered peaks as high as nine thousand feet above sea level. The beautiful scenery here attracts many tourists each year. Mountain lakes sparkle in the sun, and rivers and streams rush to the mountain valleys.

Tourists also visit the beautiful Black Forest, in the southwestern corner of Germany. This is actually a mountain range covered with dark fir trees. Quaint villages nestle in the valleys of the Black Forest and cling to the hillsides. Two important occupations in this area are lumbering and wood carving.

Rivers have cut wide, fertile valleys in the highland region of Germany.

Among these rivers are the Rhine, the Mosel, the Main, and the Neckar.

The highland region of Germany is almost as densely populated as the lowland. Valuable mineral resources here encourage industry. Rivers and mountain streams provide the transportation and waterpower necessary for manufacturing. Farming is also important in this region.

Understanding Maps

Maps are an important source of information, not only in your study of Germany, but also in everyday life. Before you can use a map skillfully, however, you need to understand some basic principles about maps. Learn about these principles by reading pages 169-176. Test your understanding by answering the following questions:

1. What system has been worked out to locate places on the earth?
2. Why is a globe more accurate than a flat map?
3. What does the term "scale of miles" mean?
4. What is the legend of a map?
5. What is meant by the earth's relief? What ways have been worked out to show relief on a map?

Using Maps

Using maps throughout your study of Germany will help you become more skillful in this activity. It will also help you understand and remember important facts about Germany. Study the maps on pages 18 and 20 and answer the following:

1. In what two land regions of Europe is Germany located?
2. What countries border East Germany? What countries border West Germany?
3. In what land region of Europe is each of the following located: Hamburg? Munich? Berlin?
4. List three important mountain ranges in Germany. Where is each located?
5. Name and locate three important rivers in Germany.

Increasing Your Understanding

Geography plays an important part in the establishment and growth of cities. Choose one of the following cities in Germany and write a report about it:

Bremen	Essen
Munich	Frankfurt am Main

In your report, tell how geographical features, such as the following, influenced the growth of the city, both in its early history and in modern times:

rivers	natural resources
mountains	the North Sea

You can refer to the suggestions on pages 178 and 179 to help you find information. The suggestions on pages 181 and 182 will help you to organize your report.

For further understanding. Make a map to illustrate your report. Show the location of the city you have chosen. Also show the location of the geographical features, such as rivers or natural resources, that influenced its growth. You can trace a map of Germany from one of the maps in this book. These maps will also be helpful to you in locating the city and the geographical features for your map.

Sharing Your Experiences

Write a report. Imagine you are taking a trip from Hamburg to Frankfurt am Main, to Stuttgart, and then southeast to Austria. Write a report about your trip through Germany, describing the countryside. Tell how the people in different areas make a living. Use this book and other sources to find the information you need. When you have finished your report, present it to your class.

Make a map. Make a map that shows the route you have taken on your trip. You may also want to show land features such as mountains and rivers and farming and industrial areas. Be sure your map has a legend.

The North Sea, which borders much of northwestern Germany, is an arm of the Atlantic Ocean. Westerly winds that blow across the Atlantic to Germany are warmed by an ocean current called the North Atlantic Drift. They give Germany a milder climate than is common for areas so far north.

2 Climate

A Study Guide

A Problem To Solve

Germany has a milder climate than is common for a country located so far north. Why is this so? In forming hypotheses, you will need to think about the following:

a. the seas that border Europe
b. the winds that blow toward Europe

Terms To Understand

You need to know the following terms in order to read this chapter with understanding. Look up terms you do not know in the glossary of this book, a dictionary, or an encyclopedia.

equator   parallel
altitude   ocean current

See TO THE STUDENT, pages 6-7.

Most of Germany lies as far north as Canada, but Germany's climate is milder than Canada's climate. The average July temperature in Germany is seventy degrees, and the average January temperature is forty degrees. If you traveled across Germany in winter, you would find more snow and cold weather in the east than the west. In summer, the east is warmer than the west.

A warm ocean current influences Germany's climate. One key to understanding the climate of Germany is a warm ocean current called the North Atlantic Drift. (See page 33.) This current flows near Europe, and an arm of the current reaches into the North Sea. Westerly winds, warmed by this current, blow over the land and keep it from getting very cold in the winter. These same winds also keep the land from getting very hot in summer, for during the summer the air over the water is cooler than the air over the land. Therefore, the winds blowing in from the sea cool the land. Sea winds also bring rain to Germany.

The climate of northwestern Germany is mild. Northwestern Germany has a milder climate than other parts of Germany. This is mainly because of the

Summer weather in northwestern Germany is pleasant. Northeastern Germany, which is farther from the Atlantic Ocean, has hotter summers.

In northwestern Germany, winters are mild. Some snow falls, but it usually melts quickly. Winters in northeastern Germany are colder.

influence of the mild westerly winds. Winters here are cool and rainy. Some snow falls, but it usually melts rapidly. In the summer, the westerlies help keep the weather in the northwest pleasant. There is also adequate rainfall for farming. Grass grows especially well in this moist, mild climate. Much land is used as pastureland for dairy cattle.

The climate is more severe in the northeast than in the northwest. The westerlies have less effect on northeastern Germany, since this area is farther from the Atlantic Ocean. Here the winters are colder and the summers hotter than in the northwest. Icy winter winds from the northeast blow over the plains.

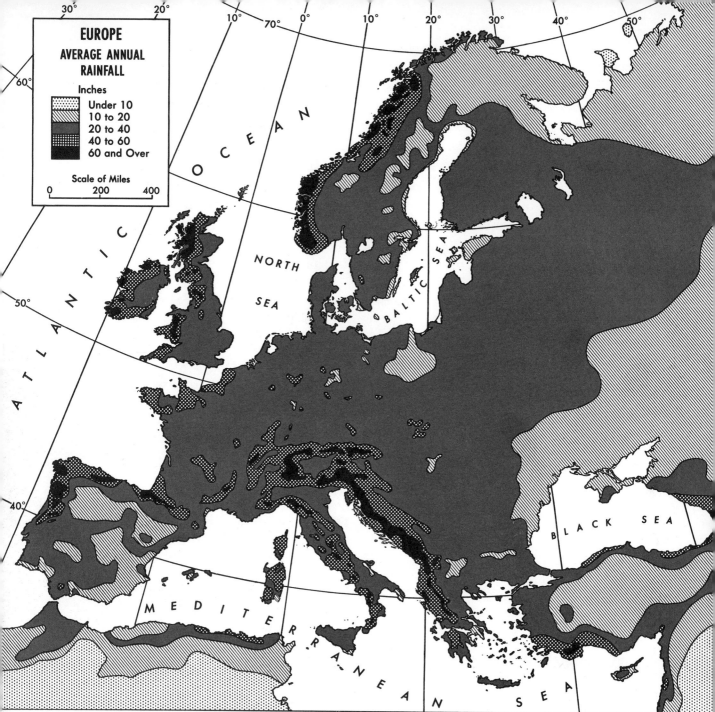

EUROPE
AVERAGE ANNUAL RAINFALL

Inches

Under 10
10 to 20
20 to 40
40 to 60
60 and Over

Scale of Miles
0   200   400

ATLANTIC OCEAN

NORTH SEA

BALTIC SEA

MEDITERRANEAN SEA

BLACK SEA

Europe's rainfall. Like much of Europe, Germany receives adequate rainfall. Some of the areas of heaviest rainfall in Germany are in the Bavarian Alps, the Black Forest, and the Harz Mountains. Moisture-filled winds that rise to cross these highlands are cooled, and lose much of their moisture in the form of rain or snow.

They make northeastern Germany one of the coldest parts of Germany in winter. However, even here, temperatures are less severe than in similar inland areas in the United States. (See page 20.)

Differences in elevation cause variations in southern Germany's climate. In southern Germany, the elevation of the land is the most important key to understanding the climate. When the moisture-laden winds rise to cross the hills and

28

mountains of southern Germany, they are cooled. Then much of the moisture in them falls as rain or snow. When the winds blow down the other side of the mountains, they are warmed again and take up moisture instead of releasing it. Thus, the mountains and hills receive more rainfall than the valleys. Some of the areas of heaviest rainfall in Germany are in the Bavarian Alps, the Black Forest, and the Harz Mountains.

The elevation of the land not only affects the amount of rainfall but also affects temperatures. These changes in temperature occur because the air is thinner and cleaner at high altitudes.* Air that is thin and clean is not able to hold the sun's heat as well as the dense, dusty air at lower altitudes. Consequently, the temperatures in the mountains and hills are generally cooler than in the valleys.

*See glossary

In the southern highlands, the climate varies with the altitude. Fruit trees are in bloom on the lower slopes when the high peaks are still covered with snow. The valleys in this part of Germany have long, pleasant summers.

Pressure Belts and Ocean Currents

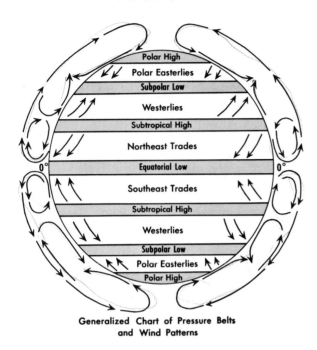

Polar High
Polar Easterlies
Subpolar Low
Westerlies
Subtropical High
Northeast Trades
Equatorial Low
Southeast Trades
Subtropical High
Westerlies
Subpolar Low
Polar Easterlies
Polar High

0°   0°

Generalized Chart of Pressure Belts and Wind Patterns

Winds. The climate of Europe is affected by winds called the westerlies. To understand how the westerlies are formed, it is necessary to study the major wind patterns of the world.

Some facts to remember about air. Before we begin to study the formation of these wind patterns, we should review some facts about air. First of all, air has weight. It presses against all surfaces with weight called atmospheric pressure. Second, warm air is lighter than cold air. When air is warmed, it expands. As it expands, it exerts less pressure on a surface, or grows lighter. It also begins to rise. You know that warm air rises if you have watched small particles of ash swept upward with the heat from a bonfire. On the other hand, when air cools, it contracts. As it contracts, it grows heavy and sinks, exerting more pressure on a surface. The rising and falling of air caused by heat, or by a lack of heat, creates air currents.

The formation of the world's wind patterns. Experts do not agree on how the world's wind patterns are formed. However, the explanation generally given is based on differences between the warm and cool areas on the earth's surface. The equator receives more direct rays of sunshine during the year than any other part of the earth's surface. These rays warm the land and water, which in turn warm the air. The warm air expands, exerts less pressure on the earth's surface, and begins to rise. Therefore, near the equator there is a low-pressure area, called the equatorial low-pressure belt.

At a high altitude, the warm air that has risen from the equatorial low-pressure belt divides into two parts. One part flows slowly

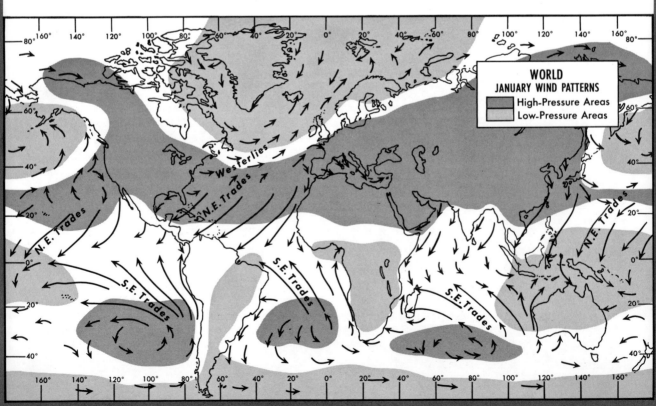

WORLD
JANUARY WIND PATTERNS
High-Pressure Areas
Low-Pressure Areas

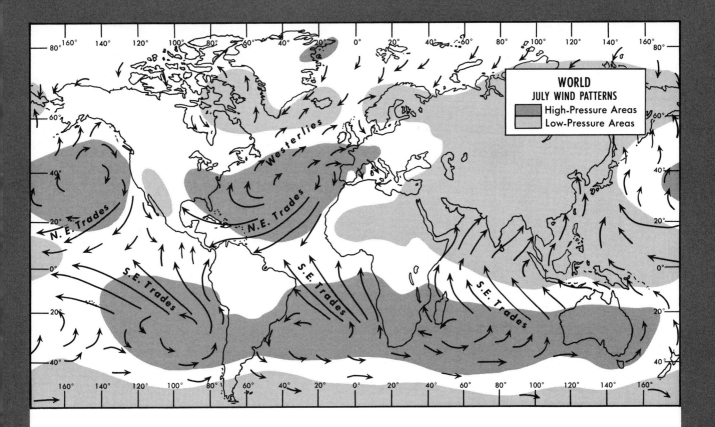

toward the North Pole, while the other flows toward the South Pole. Between the 25 and 30 degree parallels, these warm air masses become cooler and begin to sink, exerting greater pressure on the earth's surface. Therefore, the area near the 30 degree parallel in each hemisphere is called the subtropical high-pressure belt. (See chart on opposite page.)

As the warm air cools and sinks in the subtropical high-pressure belt, it again divides and moves in two directions. In each hemisphere, some currents flow toward the nearest pole, and others flow back toward the equator. The air currents that flow toward the poles are called the westerly winds, or the westerlies. The air currents that flow toward the equator are called the trade winds, or the trades.

At the North and South poles, the sun's rays are very slanted and bring little heat to the land and water. The cold, heavy air forms high-pressure areas called the polar highs. Air currents flowing from the polar highs, called the polar easterlies, travel toward the equator and meet the westerlies at about the 60 degree parallels. As they meet, they form the subpolar lows.

It is important to remember that the pressure belts are not formed as evenly as the chart on the opposite page shows. It is also important to remember that the winds mentioned are only the general wind patterns of the world. Within these patterns are many variations.

Wind direction. As you study the chart on page 30, notice that the westerlies do not blow directly toward the poles, and that the trades do not blow directly toward the equator. This is caused mainly by the fact that points on the earth's surface at the equator are moving through space much faster than points at the poles. Take a string and stretch it around a globe first at the equator and then at the 60 degree parallel. The distance around the earth at the 60 degree parallel is slightly more than one half the distance around the earth at the equator. Therefore, any given point at the equator must travel more than 1,000 miles per hour to make a complete rotation in 24 hours, while any given point at the 60 degree parallel travels only 520 miles per hour to make the same rotation.

Now imagine the westerlies blowing from the 30 degree parallel in the Northern Hemisphere. Although the westerlies are moving northward, they are also a part of the atmosphere that is moving from west to east with the rotation of the earth. At the 30 degree parallel, this speed of rotation is about 900 miles per hour. As the westerlies move northward, they tend to keep this eastward speed. The farther northward the winds blow, however, the more slowly the land

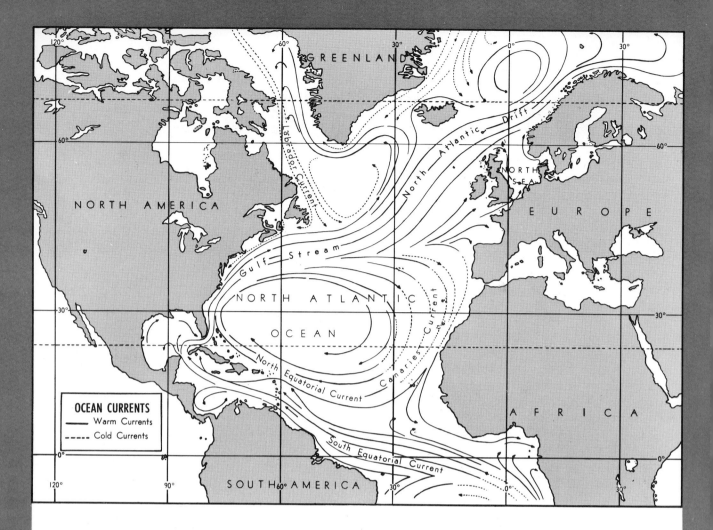

OCEAN CURRENTS
— Warm Currents
---- Cold Currents

beneath them is rotating, so that the westerlies are moving eastward faster than the land. Because their eastward movement is faster than the earth's surface beneath them, the westerlies seem to blow generally from west to east.

The earth's rotation affects the trade winds in a similar manner. Imagine the trades in the Northern Hemisphere as they blow from the 30 degree parallel toward the equator. The trades tend to keep the eastward speed of the atmosphere at the 30 degree parallel. Along their way toward the equator, however, the land beneath them rotates faster than the trades' eastward movement. Because the trades are moving eastward more slowly than the land beneath them, they seem to blow generally toward the west.

Other factors that influence wind direction. There are many other factors that influence the direction of the winds. One is the changing of the seasons. In July, the direct rays of the sun are north of the equator, and in January they are south of the equator. Since the equatorial low-pressure belt moves to where the sun's rays bring the most heat, the equatorial low-pressure belt lies farther north in July than

it does in January. Pressure belts also move because of unequal heating of land and water. Because an ocean is warmer than land in winter, a low-pressure belt tends to move over an ocean in the winter and over the land in the summer.

In some parts of the world, the movement of pressure belts causes winds to blow from one direction in summer and from another direction in winter. The map of January Wind Patterns on page 30 shows the westerlies moving over the Mediterranean area. However, the map of the July Wind Patterns on page 31 shows the trade winds blowing over the Mediterranean area. This change causes the Mediterranean lands to have moist winters and dry summers, for westerlies generally carry more precipitation to this area than the trade winds.

Ocean currents. Just as air has motion called wind, water also has a flowing motion, called a current. The map above shows that currents, which flow like rivers through the rest of the ocean waters, form large circular patterns. Some of the currents are called drifts, while others are called streams. Drifts are slow, diffused currents. They extend from the surface of the sea down as far as 800 feet, and usually travel very slowly. Streams are faster than drifts and have more clearly defined boundaries. Ocean currents of both types have an important effect on the world's climates.

Prevailing winds, such as the westerlies and the trades, are the main causes of ocean currents. The waters are blown along in the direction of the winds until they near a large landmass, such as a continent. Here they divide, some currents turning left and others right. Soon after the currents divide, they are caught up again by prevailing winds, and are carried along by them until they reach another landmass and again divide. In this way circular patterns are developed.

There are several other factors that cause ocean currents. One of these is the difference in water temperature. Like cold air, cold water sinks and flows toward the equator, causing motion in the ocean depths. Warmer water rises at the equator and flows toward the poles. Still another factor that causes motion is the difference in salt content of the water in various parts of the oceans. Water with low salt content tends to flow over water which has a high salt content and is therefore heavier.

The pattern of North Atlantic currents. The ocean currents that affect the climate of western Europe are part of a large pattern of North Atlantic currents. Locate the South Equatorial Current on the map on the opposite page. This current, heated by the tropical sun, moves westward with the trades. As it nears South America, the current divides, part turning to the northwest and part to the southwest. The northwest portion then merges with a portion of the North Equatorial Current, forming the Caribbean Current. This current flows through the Caribbean Sea and the Gulf of Mexico. As it flows out of the gulf and travels northeastward into the Atlantic Ocean it becomes the Gulf Stream.

The Gulf Stream, which is about 50 miles wide and 1,500 feet deep as it flows out of the Gulf of Mexico, is like a huge river. Its flow of water is 1,000 times greater than that of the Mississippi River. Benjamin Franklin first charted the course of the Gulf Stream. He also recorded its speed and temperature, which are known today to be about 5 miles an hour and 83 degrees as the stream passes the tip of Florida.

Soon after the Gulf Stream begins to flow along the Atlantic coast of North America, it is directed eastward toward Europe by the westerly winds. As it travels toward this continent, the current divides. Part of it goes southward and back into the tropical seas, while the other part flows northward as the North Atlantic Drift. The warm waters of the drift spread along the western coasts of Great Britain and Norway. They also warm the westerlies, which moderate the climate in much of Europe. As the drift travels farther northward, it gradually cools, mixes with other parts of the ocean, and is lost.

A farmhouse in Holland. Mild westerly winds bring enough rain for farming to much of Europe.

Checking Your Understanding

Give at least one reason that explains why each of the following is true:

1. The northwestern part of Germany has an especially mild climate.
2. The northeastern part of Germany has hotter summers and colder winters than the northwestern part.
3. The mountains in southern Germany generally receive more rainfall than the valleys.
4. The temperature in the mountains is usually cooler than in the valleys.

Increasing Your Understanding

A simple scientific experiment can help you understand one of the important concepts involved in a subject as complex as the formation of winds. You need to know that air has weight. It presses against all surfaces with weight called atmospheric pressure. You also need to know that warm air is lighter than cold air. When air is warmed, it expands. As it expands, it exerts less pressure on a surface, or grows lighter. It also begins to rise. On the other hand, when air cools it contracts. As it contracts, it grows heavy and sinks, exerting more pressure on a surface. The difference in pressure creates wind. The experiment outlined below will show that air rises when heated and sinks when cooled.

Materials needed
   a gallon jar with a wide mouth
   a short, thick candle
   petroleum jelly
   matches

Steps to follow
1. Coat the wick of the candle with petroleum jelly.
2. Light the candle.
3. Turn the jar upside down over the burning candle.

Results to note
   The smoke rises to the top of the inverted jar. It then moves along the top, down the sides of the jar to the bottom, and back to the candle.

Conclusions
   The burning candle heats the air above it. This warm air expands, grows lighter, and rises. Its path is shown by the smoke. When the warm air reaches the cool glass at the top, it is cooled. The air then contracts, grows heavier, and sinks to the bottom. There it replaces the warm rising air, and the cycle is repeated.

When you have completed the experiment, discuss with your class how this knowledge helps to explain the formation of high- and low-pressure areas. (See pages 30-33.) Before your discussion begins, refer to the suggestions on page 184.

For Further Understanding

One of the main factors that cause ocean currents is the difference in water temperature. Since warm water, like warm air, rises, motion or currents are created. The experiment outlined below shows that warm water rises.

Materials needed
   two milk bottles
   food coloring
   hot and cold water
   a small piece of poster board

Steps to follow
1. Fill one milk bottle with cold water.
2. Put several drops of food coloring into the second bottle and fill it with hot water. The water must be colored brightly to make the experiment effective.
3. Press the piece of poster board firmly against the mouth of the bottle containing cold water.
4. Invert the bottle of cold water and place its mouth directly over the mouth of the bottle containing hot water.
5. Slide the poster board carefully out from between the two bottles.

Results to note
   The hot, colored water moves upward into the cold water.

Conclusion
   Warm water rises.

Part 2
History and Government

World War II ruins in Nuremberg

The Bundestag, one of West Germany's two national lawmaking assemblies

ERLAND FRIEDEN SOZ

A meeting of the Communist-run Socialist Unity Party in East Germany

Germany has helped to shape the course of European history. In turn, Germany has been shaped by events in other countries. The two world wars, which brought great destruction and suffering to the world, were started partly because of Germany's desire for land and power. Germany became a divided country with two governments after its defeat in World War II. It is still divided today.

Germanic tribesmen were living in the land that today is Germany before Christ was born. They kept flocks of sheep and herds of cattle, and cleared land around their little villages for farming. Women, children, and slaves did the farming, while the men hunted and fought.

3 Germany to 1871

A Study Guide

Problems To Solve

1. Germany became a unified country much later than most of the other countries in Europe. <u>Why did it take the Germans so long to unite?</u> The following questions suggest some hypotheses:
   a. What part did religious conflicts play in keeping Germans divided?
   b. What part did the rulers of the different German states play in keeping Germany divided?
2. <u>How has Germany been affected by the fact that it was unified later than</u> <u>other nations?</u> Chapters 4 and 5 contain additional information that will be helpful in solving this problem.

Terms To Understand

You need to know the following terms in order to read this chapter with understanding. Look up terms you do not know in the glossary of this book, a dictionary, or an encyclopedia.

city-state	monastery
clergy	Reformation
Middle Ages	liberals
medieval	reactionaries

See TO THE STUDENT, pages 6-7.

Germany in Tribal Days

Early Germanic tribes. Twenty-five hundred years ago, forests and marshes covered much of the land where German farms and cities stand today. At that time Germany and the other present-day countries of Europe did not exist. Most of the continent was inhabited by primitive tribesmen. Among these were tribes of Germanic people who lived in Scandinavia and along the southern shore of the Baltic Sea.

About this time, large numbers of Germanic tribesmen began to move out of their homeland into the region between the Rhine and Elbe rivers. Many of the Germanic invaders stayed in this territory, but some moved on to other parts of Europe.

The Germanic people lived in tribal groups, separated by forests and marshland. They kept flocks of sheep and herds of cattle, and cleared land around their little villages to make fields for farming. The farming was done by women and children, who were helped by slaves captured in battle. The men preferred fighting and hunting to farming. They followed their chieftains into battle singing loud songs to pagan gods.

Germanic tribesmen and the Roman Empire. About the time that Germanic tribesmen were moving into what is now Germany, the city-state of Rome, in the part of Europe we now call Italy, was becoming important. As the years passed, the Romans became highly civilized. Impressive public buildings, stone bridges, and paved roads were built. The Romans also established a good system of law, a well-organized government, and a powerful army. They conquered vast territories and built up one of the greatest empires the world has ever known. Much of western Europe was included in this empire. (See map on page 38.)

The Romans established trading posts in what is now Germany, but most of this territory remained outside the Roman Empire. During the centuries that the Romans were bringing order and civilization to other parts of western Europe, many Germanic tribesmen settled in the empire. Some were captives who became farm workers. Others were

Germanic tribesmen defeated the Romans in Teutoburg Forest in A.D. 9. This discouraged Rome from taking over Germanic lands beyond the Rhine River.

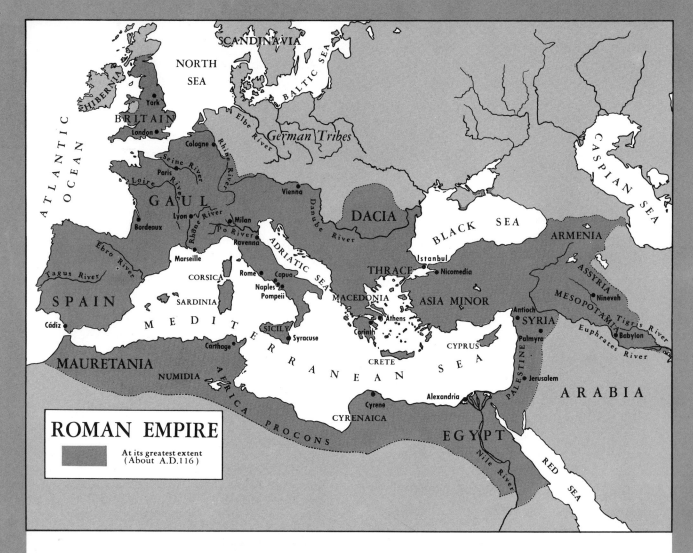

ROMAN EMPIRE
At its greatest extent
(About A.D. 116)

One of the world's greatest empires was established by the people of Rome, a city-state in what is now Italy. At its height, this empire included the lands that encircle the Mediterranean Sea and extended as far north as the northern part of Britain. In the third and fourth centuries A.D., Rome began to grow weak. By A.D. 476, Germanic tribes had overrun the western part of the empire, and Germanic chieftains had begun to establish kingdoms of their own.

soldiers who offered their services to the Roman army. Most Germanic tribesmen remained outside the empire, however, and continued to follow their primitive way of life.

Germanic tribesmen overrun the Roman Empire. In the third and fourth centuries A.D., the mighty Roman Empire began to grow weak. During the fourth century, savage tribesmen from Asia, called the Huns, began to invade Europe. They forced the Germanic tribesmen to flee before them. As time went on, thousands of Germans entered the Roman Empire, and Germanic chieftains began to take over parts of the empire. By the latter part of the fifth century A.D., the power of Rome had been destroyed.

Germany in the Middle Ages

The Middle Ages. The fall of Rome ended a period sometimes called ancient times. The period that followed is known as the Middle Ages. It lasted about one thousand years.

There was no law or order in western Europe during the early part of the Middle Ages. Fields became overgrown with weeds. Roads and bridges were not repaired. Travel and trade between cities became difficult. Bandits and thieves roamed the countryside and tribal rulers fought each other for land and power. Some of the tribal rulers built up kingdoms through their conquests. The governments of these kingdoms were usually too weak to keep order, however.

The feudal system develops. The warfare and disorder in western Europe helped to bring about a way of life called the feudal system. Under the feudal system, powerful nobles ruled parts of their king's land as their own. In return, the nobles offered military service to the kings. To help protect their lands, many nobles built up armies of lesser nobles, offering them protection and land in return for their services. The nobles' lands were worked by peasants, who received protection and the right to raise food for themselves in return for the work they did.

The life of a great noble was very different from that of the peasants. He and his family lived with their servants in a large stone castle. Often the noble entertained his friends with a banquet in the vast dining hall. Sometimes the court jester or traveling performers amused the guests while they feasted. The peasants, however, lived in wooden huts. Their meals were meager, and their lives were hard. They worked the fields with wooden plows drawn by oxen.

The influence of the Church. Although the life of a noble differed greatly from that of a peasant, there was one organization that touched the lives of all the people. This was the Christian Church. The Church's message of heavenly peace and hope brought great comfort to nobles and peasants alike in this period of fear and disorder. It is not surprising, therefore, that the Church became a unifying influence during the Middle Ages.

A castle in the Middle Ages. During the Middle Ages, governments were weak, and there was much warfare. Castles were built for protection.

In addition to creating some unity during this period, the Church performed other services. It helped crude tribesmen whose ancestors had overrun the empire to change some of their primitive ways. It also helped to keep learning alive during the years when life was too disorderly for most people to think about learning. Monks living in monasteries continued to study and to write. Thanks to them, much learning from earlier times was saved.

As you learned earlier, the Middle Ages lasted for about one thousand years in western Europe. Many events took place during this period. The following pages discuss some of the important happenings in Germany.

Charlemagne unites most tribes of Germany. About 250 years after the Middle Ages began, a king came to power who was to unite most tribes in what is now Germany. This king is known to French-

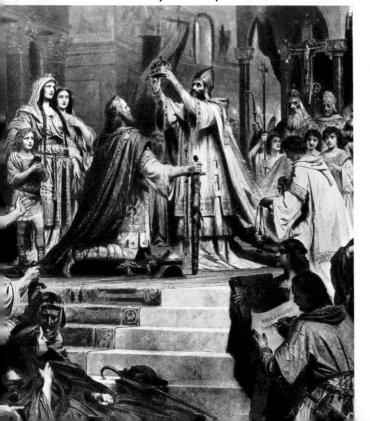

Charlemagne being crowned by the Pope. Charlemagne united under his rule most tribes in much of what is now Germany. His empire later was divided.

and English-speaking people as Charlemagne. To the Germans he is known as Karl der Grosse. Both names mean "Charles the Great."

Charlemagne was the king of a group of German tribes called the Franks. His ancestors had invaded the part of the Roman Empire that today is the country of France, and had been converted to Christianity. Charlemagne, a man of great natural intelligence, had a deep respect for learning. During his rule, he invited the most learned men in Europe to teach in a school that he established in his palace, and ordered other schools to be set up in monasteries and churches.

Charlemagne was a fearless military leader also. When he came to power, western Europe was divided and disorganized. During his lifetime, however, he united all of France and part of Italy and Spain under his rule. He also gained control of most tribes living in what is now Germany. Charlemagne forced the tribesmen who still worshiped pagan gods to accept Christianity. Under his rule, the Germans had their first opportunity to live together as citizens of a unified, orderly land.

Germany becomes a kingdom. About thirty years after the death of Charlemagne, his empire was divided among his three grandsons. The eastern part later grew to be Germany. For a time, this kingdom was ruled by descendants of Charlemagne. They were not strong rulers, however, and could not keep order.

About this time warlike invaders were raiding western Europe. Since the king of Germany was unable to protect his people, great noblemen called dukes took over this responsibility. Each duke was the protector of a large territory called a dukedom. The people in these territories soon came to feel that the dukes were their real rulers rather than the king.

When the last of Charlemagne's male descendants in Germany died, a group of dukes selected a duke to be king. This first elected king of Germany had little control, for the dukes who had chosen him felt that they were his equals. The second king, however, won the respect of the dukes by leading successful campaigns against the invaders who were threatening Germany's borders. He also took the first step toward weakening the dukes' power by granting land and privileges to the Church and to lesser noblemen called counts. The weakening of the power of the dukes greatly strengthened the power of the German king.

A German king is crowned Holy Roman Emperor. Under the third elected king, Otto I, Germany became the greatest power in Europe. Otto brought part of what is now Italy under his control. In 962 he was crowned Holy Roman Emperor by the Pope. For almost 850 years afterward, German kings used this title. During the early part of this period, the Holy Roman emperors were so powerful they could choose the man they wanted to be pope. In this way, they were able to control the Roman Catholic Church.

The Holy Roman emperors lose their power. The Holy Roman emperors did not keep their power long. By 1250, they no longer controlled northern Italy, and they had no real power in Germany.

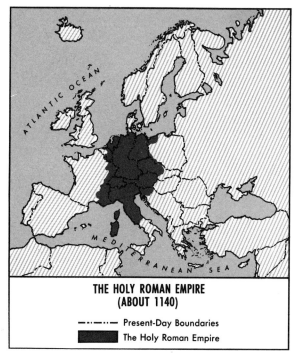

THE HOLY ROMAN EMPIRE (ABOUT 1140)
–··–··– Present-Day Boundaries
■ The Holy Roman Empire

The Holy Roman Empire was established by Otto I, who was crowned Holy Roman Emperor in 962. For almost 850 years, German kings used this title.

The country had split into many almost independent territories. Some of these territories were ruled by great nobles who were powerful enough to be called princes. Other territories belonged to the Church.

The emperors lost their power partly because they tried to do more than they had the strength to do well. They were not really strong enough to rule northern Italy. In their efforts to control this territory, the emperors neglected Germany. While the emperors were away fighting in Italy, the German princes were able to build up their power.

The Roman Catholic Church also helped to weaken the power of the Holy Roman emperors. As explained earlier, the emperors controlled the Church for a while. In the eleventh century, however, the Church began a long struggle to regain its independence. The Church

A shop in a medieval town. As the Middle Ages continued, the population of Germany and other parts of Europe increased, and towns and cities grew.

was victorious in this struggle. As a result, the emperors lost much of their control over the vast lands that had been granted to the Church in Germany. Like the princes, the religious leaders who controlled Church lands grew very powerful.

The Germans move eastward. During the time that the emperors were losing their power in Germany, several other important developments were taking place. The population of the kingdom was increasing, and the amount of spare land available was decreasing. This encouraged many Germans to move to new lands east of the Elbe River. (See map on page 18.) These eastern territories were controlled by the Slavs,* who were not as advanced as the Germans.

Different classes of people in Germany took part in the move to the east. Some eastern lands were taken over by German princes. Others were taken over by religious groups, which started monasteries. Farm workers and townspeople, such as craftsmen, moved eastward, too. Slav rulers, realizing that these industrious and skilled Germans could teach the Slavic people many things, invited more Germans to come.

*See glossary

42

As the years passed, the Germans gained control of all the territory occupied by present-day East Germany and Austria, and parts of present-day Poland and Czechoslovakia. Small groups of Germans settled as far east as Latvia and Estonia.

The Middle Ages end. Changes had been taking place in Germany and other parts of Europe during the years that the Germans were moving eastward. Cities were becoming centers of education, trade, and religion. Money was coming into wider use, making it possible for people to buy products such as shoes and farm tools. With the growth of trade, prosperous craftsmen and merchants in the cities developed into a new middle class of people who were neither peasants nor nobles. As this new class grew in wealth and influence, it was able to challenge the power of the nobles. This helped to bring about the end of the Middle Ages.

In much of Europe, the changes that brought the Middle Ages to a close helped kings to establish strong national states. This did not happen in Germany, however. The following paragraphs discuss one of the main reasons why.

Religious Differences Drive the Germans Farther Apart

Martin Luther tries to reform the Roman Catholic Church. As you have learned, cities in western Europe became centers of education during the latter part of the Middle Ages. As interest in learning grew in Europe, people began to look at the world in which they lived with questioning eyes. Some of them began to wonder if their old religious beliefs were true. This helped to bring about the Reformation, a religious movement that resulted in the formation of the Protestant churches.

One of the leaders of the Reformation was a German monk named Martin Luther, who was born in 1483. He disagreed with the accepted belief that men could find forgiveness for their sins and salvation for their souls by performing good works. After many years of thoughtful study, Luther came to believe that only through faith in God could a person be saved. At first Luther did not realize how much his ideas differed from those of the Church. In 1517, however, he became involved in a dispute that later led him to break with the Roman Catholic Church.

Luther's dispute with the Roman Catholic Church was over the manner in which certain German churchmen were trying to raise money. In Luther's time, one way the Church obtained money was by selling indulgences.* Some German churchmen said that indulgences could be bought ahead of time for sins people had not yet committed. Luther felt strongly that if indulgences were used in such a way, they violated a basic teaching of Christianity. Therefore, he made a list of his ideas on the subject. According to legend, he posted these writings to the door of the church in Wittenberg, the town where he was teaching. Because there were ninety-five statements in this list, it became known

43

Martin Luther's Ninety-Five Theses. Luther was a leader of the Reformation, which destroyed the religious unity of Germany.

as the Ninety-Five Theses. Church leaders demanded that Luther take back his statements, but he refused to do so unless they showed him proof from the Bible that he was wrong.

Luther was finally excommunicated, or cut off, from the Roman Catholic Church. This was a great punishment, for the Church taught that only with the help of its priests could people find forgiveness for their sins and salvation for their souls. Luther said, however, that faith in God was all that was necessary for salvation.

Luther wrote many books explaining his beliefs. The printing press, which had come into use about 1450, made

it easy to spread his ideas. Soon he was receiving support from many parts of Germany.

One reason why Luther received so much support was that many German princes objected to the power of the Roman Catholic Church in their country. The Church had been almost like a second government in Germany ever since it had helped to destroy the power of the emperors centuries earlier. German princes had to pay taxes to the pope in Rome. In addition, they did not have as much control as they wished over the vast Church lands in their princedoms. By supporting Luther, the princes declared their independence from Rome. They also felt free to take over the Church property within their borders.

Religious warfare leaves Germany poor and divided. War eventually broke out in Germany between the Roman Catholics and the people who were protesting against the Roman Catholic Church. These people came to be known as Protestants. The struggle between Catholics and Protestants in Germany continued for twenty-five years. Then a conference was held, and a treaty was signed that gave each German prince the right to choose whether his princedom should be Catholic or should follow the teachings of Luther. The princes in the southern part of the country generally chose to remain Catholic, but most in the north became Protestants.

For about sixty years after the treaty was signed, little serious warfare took place in Germany. During this time, however, Protestantism was spreading to other parts of Europe, and religious disagreements were growing outside Germany. Inside Germany there was

Austria and Prussia

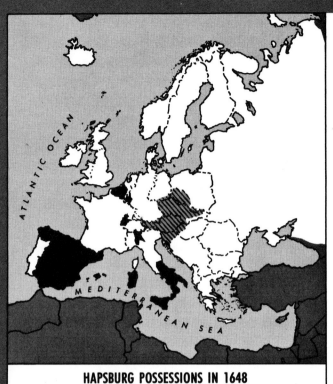

HAPSBURG POSSESSIONS IN 1648

■ Spanish Hapsburg Lands ▨ Austrian Hapsburg Lands
----- Present-Day Boundaries

At one time Germany consisted of many individual states. Important among these were Austria and Prussia.

Austria. As early as the rule of Charlemagne, Austria was important in European affairs because of its location. Austria, located in the eastern part of Charlemagne's empire, shielded the rest of the empire from neighboring peoples. Because Austria was important to the defense of Germany, the German kings who followed Charlemagne found it necessary to grant Austrian rulers more authority than the rulers of other German states.

In 1276 the rule of Austria was taken over by the Hapsburg family. By conquests, marriage alliances, and inheritances, the Hapsburgs became one of the most powerful ruling families in Europe. Through marriages the Hapsburgs inherited Spain, Luxembourg, the Netherlands, the Free County of Burgundy, and the kingdoms of Naples, Sardinia, and Sicily. In 1556, the Hapsburgs divided into two lines, the Spanish Hapsburgs and the Austrian Hapsburgs. Austria itself was the base of power of the Austrian Hapsburgs. After 1438 the leading Hapsburg in Austria was almost always chosen Holy Roman Emperor.

During the Thirty Years' War the Hapsburgs, who were Catholic, suffered defeats that weakened their power. The Treaty of Westphalia, signed at the close of the war, freed the German states from the authority of the Holy Roman Emperor and reduced the position of emperor to a mere title. With these losses, the Hapsburgs concentrated their power in Austria, Bohemia, and other surrounding possessions.

Prussia. The rise of Prussia as a military power began about 1618 with the union of two states. One of these was the state of Brandenburg in northern Germany. The other was Prussia, east of Brandenburg. Prussia was founded by an order of German knights. In 1525, a knight from the Hohenzollern family of Brandenburg took over the rule of Prussia. After the death of this knight and his son who succeeded him, the Hohenzollerns inherited Prussia and merged it with Brandenburg.

Toward the end of the Thirty Years' War, Brandenburg-Prussia grew in importance. In the treaty that ended the war, Brandenburg-Prussia won new territories. Capable rulers such as Frederick William and Frederick the Great helped to build the military power later called Prussia.

HOHENZOLLERN POSSESSIONS IN 1648

■ Hohenzollern Lands
----- Present-Day Boundaries

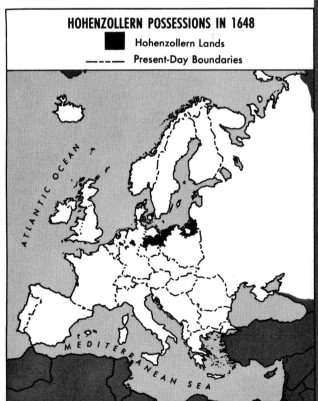

much unrest too. One cause of this unrest was the fact that princes had the right to choose the religion their people should follow.

In 1618, a group of Protestant nobles in Bohemia* tried to remove their Catholic ruler from his throne. This led to the outbreak of a series of wars between Protestants and Catholics in Europe that lasted for thirty years. Most of the countries of Europe took part in this conflict, but nearly all of the fighting was done on German soil. The Thirty Years' War left Germany a weak and broken country. When it ended, thousands of castles and villages lay in ruins, and farming and industry were practically at a standstill.

In addition to bringing destruction to Germany, the Thirty Years' War divided the country into hundreds of individual states. In the Treaty of Westphalia that was made in 1648, the different parts of Germany were given rights that made them almost independent. Each German prince was now a sovereign ruler. He had the power to govern his state as he chose and to make war or peace without asking permission of the emperor.

The Name "Germany" Disappears From the Map

For more than 150 years after the Thirty Years' War, the German states were united under an emperor in name only. In 1806, however, even this symbol of unity disappeared. To understand how this happened, we will need to learn about a man named Napoleon, who won and lost an empire in Europe.

Napoleon's rise to power. Napoleon was an army general who took advantage of the disorder during a revolution in France to come to power. This revolution was encouraged by new ideas about government, which European thinkers were discussing in the eighteenth century.

At that time, most kings in Europe ruled just as they pleased. The people they governed were generally grouped into three classes called estates. The first estate was made up of clergy and the second of nobles. These two classes did not have to pay certain heavy taxes, and enjoyed many other privileges. The third estate was made up of craftsmen, merchants, farm workers, and all other people. These people had few rights.

This system of government and society seemed wrong to some thinkers. They felt that people should enjoy equality and self-government. People who agreed with these views were known as "liberals." The success of the American Revolution, which led to the establishment of a democratic government in the United States, encouraged the spread of liberal thinking in Europe.

The French Revolution began in 1789. This revolution drove the French king and nobles from power. A time of danger and disorder followed. The French could not establish a strong, efficient government to take the place of the one they had overthrown. To make matters worse, France was involved in warfare with several foreign countries.

Queen Louise of Prussia meeting with Napoleon. At the beginning of the nineteenth century, the German states were brought under the control of the French emperor, Napoleon.

During this period of confusion, Napoleon became a popular general in the French army. The people of France began to believe that he was the one man who could defend them from their enemies and restore order to their country. They permitted him to become their dictator and supported him when he set out to conquer the rest of Europe.

Napoleon brings important changes to the German states. At the beginning of the nineteenth century, the German

NAPOLEON'S EMPIRE IN 1810

Scale of Miles

0   400   800

■ Area Under Napoleon's Control   ▨ French Allies

----- Present-Day Boundaries

Napoleon Bonaparte, the army general who brought much of Europe under his control, was born on the island of Corsica in 1769. After attending military schools in France, he joined the French army. Later, he became a leader in the revolutionary army, which was formed during the French Revolution. His brilliant military leadership and skill in administration won him the admiration and devotion of many people in France. In 1802 he was elected First Consul of France for life, and two years later he became Emperor of the French. During his reign, important political and social reforms were made in much of Europe.

The turning point in Napoleon's career came when he invaded Russia in 1812. The Russians retreated before him, but refused to surrender. Finally, outmaneuvered, Napoleon turned back, and his troops were caught in the severe Russian winter. Thousands of his men were lost, and Napoleon suffered a serious loss of prestige. By 1815, he had been driven from power by the combined forces of Britain, Prussia, and other European powers.

states were brought under Napoleon's control. Changes came to Germany while it was controlled by Napoleon. The office of Holy Roman Emperor, which had existed since Otto was crowned in 962, was abolished. Many of the smaller states were grouped together to form larger ones, and the state governments were reorganized. The French made some of these reforms. In the state of Prussia, however, government reforms were made by the Prussians themselves. The shock of being defeated by France had awakened them to the need for strengthening their state. Besides making their government more efficient, the Prussians reorganized their army.

Napoleon's defeat furthers the division of Germany. In 1814 and 1815, the com-

bined forces of Prussia and several other European powers defeated Napoleon. The European leaders who wrote the peace settlements at this time drastically changed the map of Europe. Some of the most important changes were made in Germany. Napoleon had already grouped some of the smaller states together to form larger ones. The men who redrew the map regrouped the German states until there were fewer than forty states.

The German states called themselves the German Confederation. This name had no meaning, however, for the organization that was set up to govern the confederation had no power to make the states obey its commands. From this time on, the names of the individual states began to be used on maps rather than the name "Germany."

The Germans Unite

A desire for unity grows in Germany. Napoleon's control had another effect on Germany. During the time his soldiers occupied the country, people in all the states came to realize that they were Germans who shared a common enemy. Many Germans came to feel the states should be united to form one nation. This feeling of belonging together as a nation is called nationalism.

The feeling of nationalism was not new in Germany. German thinkers had discussed uniting the German people centuries earlier. However, religious conflicts had made this impossible for many years. After Napoleon was defeated, the pride and selfishness of princes in the various German states again put an end to hopes of uniting the country. These princes feared that unity might cause them to lose some of their power and privileges. They were determined to keep their thrones even at the price of keeping the country divided.

Liberal thinkers try to unite Germany, but fail. One group of people in the German states was particularly anxious to unite the nation. This was the liberal group, made up of people who believed in democracy and the rights of man. They wanted the German states to be united under a democratic government.

For a long time after Napoleon was defeated, the German liberals could not carry out their plans. The rulers of Prussia and Austria, the two most powerful German states, were strongly opposed to democracy, for they knew it would take away their power. A powerful Austrian government official named Metternich led the fight against liberalism. Under his direction, secret police and courts were set up in most of the German states to control the liberals and to prevent revolutionary activities.

By the middle of the nineteenth century, however, the liberals throughout western Europe had gained strength. In 1848, revolutions took place in many European countries. During this year of revolutions, the liberals in every German state succeeded in overthrowing their state governments.

The liberals now had their opportunity to unite Germany under a democratic government. They arranged a

Prince Metternich, a powerful Austrian government official, helped prevent the German states from being united under a democratic government.

49

conference of representatives from all the German states. When these representatives met, however, trouble arose. They could not agree on what rights should be guaranteed by the new all-German constitution. Week after week passed while they discussed this matter. Meanwhile, the reactionaries had time to make plans about how they could restore the power of the former rulers.

In 1849, the German liberals completed their work on a German constitution. They asked the King of Prussia to become emperor of Germany and to rule according to this constitution. By this time, however, the reactionaries had succeeded in regaining their strength. Prussia's king refused the crown offered by liberals, saying that

Otto von Bismarck, chancellor of Prussia, was a nobleman opposed to democracy. He believed Prussia should unite Germany under its rule.

he would take it only from a council of princes. Both Prussia and Austria then refused to approve the constitution that the liberals had written. Without the cooperation of these two powerful states it was impossible to unite Germany. The liberals had failed.

Bismarck of Prussia unites Germany by force. Twenty-two years later, in 1871, a nobleman who strongly opposed democracy succeeded in doing what the liberals had failed to do. This man was Otto von Bismarck, chancellor of Prussia.

Bismarck firmly believed that it was Prussia's duty and right to unite the German states under Prussian leadership. He knew that the proud state of Austria would never agree to being ruled by Prussia. Therefore, the only way to carry out his plan of uniting the country would be to form a union of states that did not include Austria.

Bismarck used force to carry out his plan for uniting Germany. In 1866, he provoked Austria into a war in which Prussia speedily defeated Austria. Next, Prussia took over several neighboring German states. The remaining states north of the Main River then had no choice but to join with Prussia in forming a new union called the North German Confederation. The southern states kept their independence, but agreed to put their armies under Prussia's command if they were threatened by an outside country.

Five years later, Bismarck had an opportunity to bring the southern states into the union. France, which had grown fearful of Prussia's rising power, declared war on Prussia, and the southern German states put their armies under Prussia's command. As the war

The bombardment of Strasbourg took place in 1870, during the war between France and Germany. Many Germans developed a strong feeling of nationalism during this conflict. When the war ended in 1871, Germany was united and the King of Prussia was named German emperor.

continued, the feeling of German nationalism grew strong in these southern states. When the war ended in 1871, they agreed to join with the North German Confederation to form a single nation with the King of Prussia as its emperor. Bismarck's dream had finally become a reality.

How the events of history affected Germany. The events of history had a strong influence in shaping the type of country that Germany became. During the long years before the German states were united, great differences developed between them. Some states were mainly Catholic and others mainly Protestant. The people dressed differently and built different kinds of houses from place to place. They even spoke different dialects. (See page 131.) Improvements in transportation helped to bring people in the German states into closer contact. For a long time, many people continued to feel more loyalty to their state than to the country as a whole.

The repeated failure of the liberals to establish a democratic government also helped to shape the type of country Germany became. Many Germans came to feel that democracy was a system that could not work. They came to have more faith in a single strong leader. In later years this faith was to lead them to disaster.

The fact that Germany became a unified nation so much later than other countries had another important influence on the Germans. Other nations had already established modern industries and taken over territories in other parts of the world by the time the Germans united. The Germans were aware that they were economically behind other Western nations. The following chapter will show what effect this had on Germany and on the entire world.

TIME LINE

Decline of the Roman Empire

Beginning of the Middle Ages

The great Roman Empire begins to decline

The savage Huns invade Europe and force Germanic tribesmen southward into the Roman Empire

Germanic tribes plunder Rome

The power of Rome is destroyed

Confusion and disorder reign

| A.D.200 | A.D.300 | A.D.400 | A.D.500 | A.D.600 |

Checking Your Understanding

1. What part did Germanic tribesmen play in the fall of the Roman Empire?
2. How did the feudal system develop?
3. What were some important contributions Charlemagne made to Germanic tribes?
4. Give two reasons why the Holy Roman emperors lost much of their power by 1250.
5. What developments helped bring the Middle Ages to a close?
6. Why was Luther able to gain support for his ideas?
7. What effects did the Thirty Years' War have on Germany?
8. In what ways did Napoleon's rule and defeat bring changes to the German states?
9. Why did the liberals fail in their efforts to unite Germany?
10. How did Bismarck form the North German Confederation?
11. Why did the southern German states join the North German Confederation?
12. What effects did the repeated failure to establish democracy in Germany have on the German people?

Sharing Your Understanding

The Middle Ages includes a vast period of history from about A.D. 500 to 1500. During this time, very few changes took place in Europe. Conduct a class study of life during the Middle Ages. For this study, each student can choose a topic from the list below and write a report.

music	crusades
literature	knighthood
education	nobles
clothing	castles
drama	tournaments
guilds	religion

The suggestions on pages 178-182 will help you to find and evaluate information and to organize your report. When you have written your report you may wish to present it to the rest of the class. Pictures and drawings will make the reports more interesting. After the reports have been presented, the class may wish to review the important ideas included in the reports, and draw some conclusions about life in the Middle Ages. Each student should then organize his ideas into a brief essay on the Middle Ages.

Understanding History

In studying history, it is important to understand in what order events occurred. A time line, like the one on the opposite page, can help you see an event in relation to other events of history. Using this time line as a guide, you can make your own time line of German history. Keep in mind that many historical events cannot be confined to exact dates, but extend over long periods of time. Therefore, many events will have to be placed only in approximate order. Before preparing your time line, make a list of the important events mentioned in this chapter. Then, decide how much space you will use to represent a period of time, such as a century. You will also want to make some sketches to illustrate many of the events. As you continue your study of Germany, add more events to your time line. You may want to do this project on a large piece of poster board so that it can be used for classroom display.

Increasing Your Understanding

The men listed below have played an important part in the development of Germany. Choose one of these men and write a short biography about him.

Charlemagne	Napoleon
Otto I	Prince Metternich
Martin Luther	Otto von Bismarck

In the biography, give a brief summary of the man's life and tell what influence he had on German history. Use this book and other sources to find information. The suggestions on pages 178-182 will be helpful to you in locating and evaluating information and in writing the biography.

53

World War II ruins in Germany. During the twentieth century, two world wars brought destruction and suffering to much of the world. Germany played a leading part in these conflicts.

4 Germany Since 1871

A Study Guide

Thoughts To Help You

Germany's desire for territory and power helped to bring on two world wars. As you study this chapter, look for answers to the following questions:

1. What effects did the outcome of World War I have on Germany?
2. How did the effects of World War II differ from those of World War I?

Terms To Understand

You need to know the following terms in order to read this chapter with understanding. Look up terms you do not know in the glossary of this book, a dictionary, or an encyclopedia.

Allies	Great Depression
the Saar	Cold War
Alsace-Lorraine	NATO

The World Wars

Within this century, two wars have brought destruction and death to a large part of the world. Germany played a leading part in these global conflicts. In 1914 and again in 1939, the Germans invaded neighboring lands. Both times, the British, French, Americans, and their allies joined together to drive the Germans back. In order to understand the world wars, you need to know about Germany's history after the country was unified in 1871.

Germany becomes a leading industrial nation after 1871. Germany's business and industry grew rapidly after 1871. German scientists, businessmen, bankers, government officials, and educators worked together to help their country become a great industrial nation. They made good use of Germany's mineral resources, waterways, and forests. By 1914, ships flying the German flag were carrying German products to all parts of the world.

Industrial Germany wants more colonies. Germany's growing industries needed new places to sell their products. More colonial territories would have helped to answer this need. However, all the valuable territories had been claimed long before by other nations. The Germans did acquire some colonial territories in Africa and the Pacific, but they looked with envious eyes at the richer possessions of neighboring countries.

Germany's desire for more land alarms its neighbors. Other nations soon became alarmed by Germany's desire for land. When Germany's leaders built

one of the strongest armies in Europe, France looked on with fear. When Germany began to build a large fleet of war and merchant ships, Great Britain also grew fearful. The British could not afford to let an unfriendly power control the seas, for Great Britain needed to import food and raw materials. Largely because of Germany's actions, the nations of Europe began to prepare for war.

World War I. War came in 1914. After a four-year struggle, the Allies defeated the Central Powers, as Germany and the countries who fought with it were called. Although little fighting had taken place on German soil, the country suffered great losses. Under the terms of the peace treaty with the

Making treaty arrangements after World War I. Under the terms of the peace treaty with the Allies, Germany suffered great losses.

Exploring History With Maps

GERMANY IN 1871

NORTH SEA · DENMARK · BALTIC SEA · NETHERLANDS · RUSSIA · BELGIUM · LUX. · FRANCE · AUSTRIA-HUNGARY · SWITZERLAND

GERMANY AFTER WORLD WAR I

BALTIC SEA · DENMARK · LITH. · NORTH SEA · NETHERLANDS · POLAND · BELGIUM · LUX. · CZECHOSLOVAKIA · FRANCE · AUSTRIA · SWITZERLAND · HUNGARY

GERMAN EXPANSION IN 1939

DENMARK · BALTIC SEA · LITH. · NORTH SEA · NETHERLANDS · U.S.S.R. · BELGIUM · LUX. · FRANCE · SLOVAKIA · SWITZERLAND · HUNGARY

GERMANY TODAY

DENMARK · BALTIC SEA · NORTH SEA · NETHERLANDS · POLAND · BELGIUM · LUX. · FRANCE · SWITZERLAND

Areas Claimed by Poland and the U.S.S.R.

⌂ Berlin

Germany did not become politically unified until 1871, later than most of the other nations of Europe. Following unification, Germany rapidly became the most powerful country on the continent of Europe. The desire of Germany for land and power beyond its borders helped to bring on World War I, in which Germany was defeated by the United Kingdom, the United States, France, and their allies.

Germany lost important territories in World War I. The terms of the Treaty of Versailles, signed in 1919 after World War I, deprived the Germans of all their overseas colonial territories. In addition, important parts of Germany were lost to France and Poland. The peace treaty of 1919 caused much bitterness in Germany.

Ten years after the peace treaty of 1919, Germany was hit by the Great Depression.* During this period of hardship, a leader rose to power who promised the Germans that he would make their country prosperous and powerful again. This leader was Adolf Hitler, head of the Nazi Party. Under Hitler's leadership, Germany set out to conquer Europe. This resulted in World War II, in which Germany was again defeated.

World War II brought great destruction to Germany and left it a divided country. Until a peace treaty could be signed, the territories east of the Oder and Neisse rivers were placed under Polish and Soviet administration. The rest of the country was divided into four zones, occupied by Britain, France, the United States, and the Soviet Union. Since Cold War disputes have made reunification impossible, the three Western zones have formed West Germany. The Soviet zone has become known as East Germany.

*See glossary

Standing in line for bread after World War I. Post-war difficulties and the Great Depression helped Hitler rise to power in Germany.

Allies, the Germans lost the important industrial regions of the Saar and Alsace-Lorraine. They also lost a large industrial and agricultural region in the east. All of Germany's overseas possessions were taken away, and the Germans were forced to pay large sums of money, called reparations, to the Allies.

Germany suffers hardships after World War I. Germany had to work hard to rebuild its business and industry after World War I. Conditions were improving when the Great Depression brought hard times to the whole world. Banks failed, and people lost their money. Factories and offices closed. In Germany, as in other lands, the people suffered from hunger and unemployment.

Hitler wins the Germans' support with promises of prosperity and power. In the

midst of these troubled times, a man rose to power who promised to make Germany prosperous and powerful again. This man was Adolf Hitler, the leader of the Nazi Party. (See Chapter 5.) Hitler told the people that Germany could rule the world. He claimed that all Germans belonged to a "master race," which made them better, braver, stronger, and more intelligent than other people. He said that the chief enemies of this master race were the Jews, who should be destroyed.

Another of Hitler's dangerous teachings was that right is always on the side of the strong. He taught that it was right for Germany to attack and conquer a weaker neighbor. The fact that the Germans were strong enough to conquer was supposed to prove that they were right.

World War II ruins in Berlin. Hitler's dreams of conquest helped to bring about World War II, in which the Germans were defeated.

Many discontented people in Germany welcomed Hitler as their leader. They accepted his myth about the master race and his claim that war would bring prosperity to Germany. They did not stop him when he organized a great army and ordered factories to produce tanks, guns, and airplanes. Nor did they stop him when he had millions of Jews imprisoned and murdered in concentration camps. By the time some of the people realized that Hitler's actions would ruin Germany, it was too late. The Nazi Party controlled the lives of the people. No one could disagree openly with the government without fear of imprisonment or death.

World War II. Hitler's armies invaded neighboring lands, and again there was war. The countries that fought against the Germans were called the Allies. Germany and the countries that fought with the Germans were called the Axis powers. World War II brought terrible destruction to Germany. Large sections of German cities were destroyed. Industries were shattered, and millions of people were made homeless. With the surrender of the Nazi leaders in 1945, Germany's government collapsed.

A Divided Country

Allied plans for dividing Germany. Before World War II ended, the leaders of the main Allied nations discussed what should be done with Germany when it surrendered. There were many matters that would have to be attended to. Territories seized from neighboring countries by Hitler would have to be returned, and new boundaries would have to be drawn. Until these and other problems could be worked out, the Allies decided that Germany should be divided into several parts. Each part would be occupied by the forces of one Allied nation. The occupation forces would have the responsibility of making certain Germany did not prepare for war again.

Germany is divided. After Germany surrendered in 1945, the Allies held another conference, at the city of Potsdam, where final arrangements were made for dividing the conquered country. By this time, the Polish army had already occupied Germany east of the Oder and Neisse rivers except the easternmost part. This had been taken over by the Soviets. (See bottom map on page 56.) Until a peace treaty could be signed, the Allies agreed that the territories east of the Oder and Neisse rivers were to be temporarily controlled by Poland and the Soviet Union. The rest of Germany was temporarily divided into four zones. Britain, France, the United States, and the Soviet Union each occupied one zone. The city of Berlin, which was deep inside the Soviet zone of Germany, was temporarily divided among these Allies also. (See Chapter 6.) The four Allies formed a joint Control Authority to govern Germany until a treaty could be made and the country could be reunited under its own government.

Disagreements arise among the Allies. Plans for reuniting Germany did not work out, however. The Allies had difficulty agreeing among themselves about the terms of the peace treaty. The French, who had suffered great losses in both world wars, wanted to make certain that the Germans could never start another war. The restrictions they wanted to place on Germany in the peace treaty did not seem wise to the British and the Americans. While these plans were being worked out, disagreements began to separate the Soviet Union from the three Western powers. These disagreements were part of the growing conflict that came to be known as the Cold War.

One of the main disagreements in the Cold War was over what type of government Germany should have. The Western powers favored a democratic government, while the Soviets believed Germany should become Communist. Most Germans were strongly anti-Communist, and in the elections that were held in Germany right after the war, few Communists were chosen for public office.

When the Soviets realized that communism would not come to Germany through honest elections, they brought it by force to the eastern part of the country, which was under their control.

A border-crossing point. At the close of the war, Germany was divided into several parts. The division of Germany was meant to be temporary. However, Germany is still divided today.

(See page 88.) From there, the Soviets hoped to spread communism to the rest of Germany. Of course, the Western powers were determined to keep them from doing so. The disagreements between the Soviets and the Western powers made it impossible at this time to reach agreement on plans for reuniting Germany.

Cooperation ends between the Soviets and the Western powers. The Americans and British knew that as long as Germany was divided into small parts, it would be very difficult for the Germans to rebuild their economy. Although it was impossible at this time for all of Germany to be reunited, it was possible to join the American and British zones. In 1947, this was done. A year later, the French were persuaded to join their zone of occupation with the British and American zones. These three western

A joint meeting of the Bundestag and Bundesrat, West Germany's lawmaking assemblies. The Western powers, who occupied the western part of Germany, helped the people here establish a democratic government. West Germany became fully independent in 1955.

zones became West Germany. West Germans and the Western powers made plans to rebuild industry and to establish self-government in West Germany.

The actions of the Western powers displeased the Soviets, for now it would be difficult to bring communism to West Germany. In March, 1948, the Soviet representative walked out of the Allied Control Council, and refused to return. Next, the Soviets tried to force the Western powers out of Berlin by blocking all roads, railroads, and canals through which supplies could be brought to the city. As Chapter 6 shows, the Western powers refused to be pushed out of Berlin. For nearly a year they brought in by airplane all supplies that Berlin needed. The Berlin Blockade was ended in 1949, but by this time, the quarrel between the Soviet Union and the Western powers was so bitter that there seemed no way to end it.

The Federal Republic is formed. During the Berlin Blockade, a constitution was written for West Germany. (See page 84.) After this constitution was adopted in 1949, West Germany became known officially as the Federal Republic of Germany. In 1955, it became fully independent.

The Federal Republic of Germany is a close ally of the other Western nations that oppose communism. It is a member of NATO, and belongs to the European Community. (See page 98.) As the following chapters show, the Federal Republic has become one of the world's leading industrial powers, and its people enjoy a high standard of living. More important, it has a democratic government that permits the people to live and work in freedom.

A Communist meeting in Warsaw. East Germany and several other eastern European countries have a mutual defense treaty, the Warsaw Pact.

The Democratic Republic is formed. Shortly after the Federal Republic was formed, a constitution was adopted in East Germany, and this area declared itself to be the German Democratic Republic. Although it is called a democratic republic, East Germany is really a Communist dictatorship. (See pages 87-90.) Its Communist leaders are German, but they follow orders from the Soviet Union, whose soldiers help to keep them in power. The Democratic Republic carries on most of its trade with the Communist countries of eastern Europe. In 1955, together with several other eastern European Communist nations, it signed a mutual defense treaty called the Warsaw Pact.

As the chapters that follow show, the government of East Germany controls the people's lives. Living conditions under the Communists are so unpleasant that millions of East Germans have fled to West Germany. To prevent more people from escaping, the East German government has built watchtowers and barbed-wire fences along the border between the two Germanys. In Berlin, it has built a wall. (See pictures on pages 73 and 76.) Even so, desperate East Germans still risk their lives to live in freedom.

Divided Germany today. The Allies still have not signed a peace treaty with the Germans. At times, the Soviet Union has threatened to sign a separate peace treaty with the East German government, but it has not done so yet. In the meantime, Germany remains divided. (See bottom map on page 56.) Poland and the Soviet Union say that Germany no longer has any right to the territories east of the Oder and Neisse rivers, and the East German government has agreed to give them up. The West German government, however, says that these territories are rightfully a part of Germany. Many Germans still hope for the day Germany will be reunited, but there seems little chance that this will happen as long as the Cold War continues.

Checking Your Understanding

1. What losses did Germany suffer as a result of World War I?
2. How did Hitler gain the support of the Germans?
3. Why was Germany divided after World War II?
4. What disagreements between the Allies prevented Germany from being reunited?
5. What events led to the formation of the Federal Republic of Germany in 1949?
6. What are some of the basic differences between the Federal Republic of Germany and the German Democratic Republic?

Understanding History

Continue the time line that you began in Chapter 3 by adding the important events covering the period of time discussed in this chapter.

For further understanding. Compare the development of the United States with that of Germany by adding important events in American history to your time line. For example, about the time Martin Luther posted his Ninety-Five Theses, explorers were just beginning to come to America. You can begin this project by making a list of events in American history and their dates that you wish to add to your time line. You will want to be sure to distinguish events in American history from events in German history. However, you may prefer to make a separate time line for events in American history. If you do this, be sure that the time lines cover the same period of time in order to help you compare the development of the United States with that of Germany.

Sharing Your Knowledge

Throughout history, man has spent much of his time, energy, and resources in waging war. However, these wars often created more conflicts than they settled. As a class, you may want to discuss the following questions:

1. How did the problems that were left unsettled after World War I help cause World War II?
2. How could the problems that have been left unsettled since World War II lead to a third world war?

Before you begin your class discussion, refer to the suggestions on pages 183 and 184 to help make your discussion successful. Also, refer to the suggestions on pages 178-180 to help you locate information for your class discussion.

Adolf Hitler in a motorcade

Walter Ulbricht reviewing a parade

Two dictators have come to power in Germany during the twentieth century. The first was Adolf Hitler, whose Nazi Party controlled Germany from 1933 until 1945. The second, Walter Ulbricht, is the head of Communist East Germany.

5 Two Dictatorships

A Study Guide

A Problem To Solve

From 1933 to 1945, Germany was ruled by the Nazi Party, headed by the dictator Adolf Hitler. <u>What made it possible for a dictator to come to power in Germany?</u> In forming hypotheses, you will want to consider answers to the following questions:

1. How does Germany's earlier history help to explain why a dictator was able to come to power here?

2. What events and conditions following World War I helped Hitler come to power?

Terms To Understand

You need to know the following terms in order to read this chapter with understanding. Look up terms you do not know in the glossary of this book, a dictionary, or an encyclopedia.

dictatorship   nationalism
communism   propaganda

See TO THE STUDENT, pages 6-7

Twice during this century, dictatorships have been established in Germany. The first was set up by Adolf Hitler in 1933 and lasted until his armies surrendered to the Allies in 1945. The second was established by Communists in East Germany, and is still in power. It is worthwhile for the citizens of a democracy to ask, "How was it possible for both Hitler and the Communists to come to power in Germany?" This question is partially answered in Chapter 4. It will be considered further in the paragraphs that follow.

Adolf Hitler's early life. Adolf Hitler, the leader who established the first of Germany's two dictatorships, was born in 1889, in Austria. His father was a minor government official. Although his father hoped that young Hitler would choose a similar type of work, Adolf wanted to be an artist. He took little interest in his studies, however, and left school when he was sixteen.

During the next few years, Hitler made little effort to find work. He tried twice to enroll in the Academy of Arts in Vienna, but his drawings were considered so poor that he was not admitted. Other than this, Hitler made no effort to continue his formal education.

When Hitler was nineteen, his mother died, and he moved to Vienna. The following years were among the hardest of his life. He was not prepared for any vocation and did not try to find steady work. Instead, he earned a poor living by doing odd jobs such as shoveling snow and painting advertising posters.

During this period of aimlessness and frustration, Hitler read a great deal and observed life around him. As he was to later write in his book *Mein Kampf:**

"In this period there took shape within me a world picture and a philosophy which became the granite foundation of all my acts. In addition to what I then created, I have had to learn little; and I have had to alter nothing."

Hitler's beliefs. The philosophy that Hitler developed is so foolish and fantastic that today it is almost impossible to take it seriously. Nevertheless, it is important to know about the ideas that resulted in the deaths of millions of innocent people and led a nation to disaster. Hitler believed that mankind could be classified into superior and inferior races. He felt that history was the story of struggle between higher and lower races for survival and mastery. According to Hitler, the highest of the races was what he called the "Aryan" or "Germanic" race. Hitler believed that all the important achievements in history had been made by this so-called master race. He also believed that the chief enemies of the "master race" were the Jewish people. According to Hitler, the Jews were trying to take advantage of democracy and communism to achieve world power.

Hitler felt that the Germanic peoples of both Austria and Germany belonged to the "master race." He believed, however, that the Germanic people of Austria had been weakened by the many people in the Austrian Empire who belonged to non-Germanic races. Therefore, his main interest was centered in Germany.

Hitler believed that the Germanic peoples should unite behind an all-powerful leader who would rule for the benefit of their race. Once a truly Germanic state had been established in

*See glossary

Germany, it should be expanded to include the other Germanic peoples of Europe. Then the Germans should set out to conquer the "lesser" races of Europe and of the world.

How Hitler put his beliefs into action. Hitler's strong feeling of German nationalism encouraged him to volunteer for the German army during World War I. When he received news of Germany's defeat, he was stunned. Unable to believe that the Germans could be conquered in a fair fight, he became convinced that they had been "stabbed in the back" by Jews and Communists at home. While still in the army, he resolved to enter politics and personally return Germany to what he believed was its rightful place in world leadership.

Hitler first planned to form a political party of his own, but instead he joined one of the many small political groups that were formed in Germany after World War I. His talents as a speaker and organizer soon made him leader of the group, which in time became the National Socialist, or Nazi, Party.

The Nazi Party did not become powerful until the Great Depression. During this time of unemployment and misery, Hitler cleverly took advantage of the confusion and despair that many people in Germany felt. Hitler's accusations against the Jews gave people someone to blame for their troubles. In addition, Hitler's promises for German prosperity and world power gave them hope.

Hitler and President von Hindenburg. Hitler's Nazi Party became powerful during the Great Depression, which brought widespread unemployment and suffering to Germany. In January, 1933, President von Hindenburg appointed Hitler to the high position of chancellor.

Hitler speaking to the Reichstag, the lawmaking assembly of Germany. In March, 1933, the Reichstag voted to give Hitler powers that made him dictator of Germany.

The Germans showed their approval of Hitler by electing large numbers of his Nazi Party to the *Reichstag,* the lawmaking assembly of Germany. In 1932, the Nazi Party became the largest political party in the *Reichstag.* However, the other political parties combined had more members in this assembly than the Nazis. For a while, this prevented Hitler from obtaining the unlimited power he needed to carry out his plans.

To gain the power he wanted, Hitler used trickery and force. At the same time that he was promising to improve the working conditions of factory laborers, he was secretly making very different promises to powerful leaders of industry. He led these industrialists to believe that if they would support him,

they would be allowed to run their factories as they pleased when he came to power. Hitler also made promises to the German army. He knew that many officers were dissatisfied because Germany had been forced to cut down the size of its army after World War I. Hitler declared that when he came to power, the army would regain its glory. Because of his promises, many army leaders and some wealthy industrialists pressured President von Hindenburg* into appointing Hitler chancellor.

When Hitler became chancellor, the Nazis still had fewer members in the *Reichstag* than the other political parties combined. Hitler knew this would make it difficult for him to obtain the unlimited power he wanted. Hoping to get more Nazis elected to the *Reichstag,* he arranged for new elections to be held. During the campaign for this election, Hitler used his powers as chancellor to help the Nazi Party. Radio stations were allowed to broadcast only the campaign speeches of Nazi leaders. The Nazis set up loudspeakers in the squares and held impressive torchlight parades. In addition, Hitler's private army, the brown-shirted storm troopers, forcibly broke up the meetings of opposing political parties. During the period of violence and terror that preceded the elections, dozens of anti-Nazis were beaten up or murdered. Also, the *Reichstag* building was mysteriously burned. The Nazis blamed the *Reichstag* fire on one of their main opponents, the German Communist Party, hoping that this would frighten the people into believing that the Communists were on the verge of taking over the country by force.

In spite of Hitler's efforts, too few Nazis were elected to give him the power he wanted. To solve this problem, Hitler had many of his opponents in the *Reichstag* arrested. Then most of the men who were left voted to give him the powers that made him dictator of Germany.

Hitler used the powers voted to him by the *Reichstag* to force the people to do as he wanted. The police were ordered to arrest all persons who opposed him. Many of these persons were put in prisons or concentration camps, where they were tortured or killed. By ruthlessly crushing all who opposed them, the Nazis hoped to discourage the people from even thinking about resistance.

To obtain the goods needed to prepare Germany for war, Hitler's government made laws controlling farming and industry. Farmers and factory owners were told what to produce and how much to deliver to the government. Factory workers could change jobs only with government approval.

Hitler also used his powers to gain control of the people's minds. He wanted them to follow him blindly. The Nazis set out to achieve this goal by taking over the press and radio. The people were told only what the government wanted them to believe. The propaganda they heard and read made Hitler seem like a god. The Nazis even tried to force churches to follow Nazi commands. Church leaders who refused to do so were imprisoned.

A Nazi rally. Hitler wanted the Germans to follow him blindly. Nazi propaganda was designed to gain control of the people's minds.

The Nazis also used the schools to spread their propaganda. Textbooks that had been used before the Nazis took over were burned. These were replaced with books that presented Hitler's teachings. Sometimes storm troopers came to the schools and questioned teachers in front of their pupils. Teachers who were failing to teach Hitler's beliefs were arrested. Hitler also used the schools as a means of training young people to obey orders without thinking. He did not want German children to develop the ability to think for themselves, since this might have led them to question Nazi teachings.

Hitler's dictatorship lasted nearly twelve and one-half years. As Chapter 4 helps to explain, it came to an end when Nazi Germany was defeated in World War II. Since that time, democracy has been restored in West Germany. Chapter 7 describes the democratic rights and freedoms West Germans now enjoy. In East Germany, however, a new dictatorship has been established.

A dictatorship imposed by outsiders. Unlike the Nazis, the Communists in East Germany were brought to power by soldiers from a foreign country. The Soviet army, which occupied eastern Germany after World War II, forced the people to accept Communist leadership. (See Chapter 4.) When the East Germans revolted in 1953, Soviet tanks were brought in to put down this uprising.

The Communist dictatorship of East Germany is like the Nazi dictatorship

Soviet tanks were brought in to put down an East German revolt in 1953. East Germany's Communist dictatorship was brought to power by Soviet occupation forces.

in many ways. The Communists have forced the people to surrender their rights and freedoms. The people have no voice in deciding how their state should be run, and may be punished for opposing government policies. Newspapers, radio stations, schools, and churches are under government control. Farming, industry, and other branches of the economy also are controlled by the government. Communist control of the economy goes beyond that of the Nazis, however. The Nazis forced private farmers and manufacturers to follow government orders, but the Communist government has actually taken over farms and industries. The restrictions that the Communists have forced on the people of East Germany have made life so unpleasant that millions of East Germans have fled westward to live in freedom. This led the Communists to build the Berlin Wall, symbol of East Germany's enslavement.

Checking Your Understanding

1. What was Hitler's philosophy regarding race?
2. How did the Great Depression help the Nazi Party gain power?
3. What measures were used by the Nazis to overcome opposing political parties?
4. List three measures used in Nazi Germany to control people's thinking.
5. In what ways did the Nazis control the economy of Germany?
6. How did the Communists come to power in eastern Germany?

Increasing Your Understanding

Although generalizations* are an important part of learning, they must be used very carefully and be supported by facts. Below are several generalizations about dictatorships. Using each of these generalizations as a topic sentence, write a paragraph for each. You will want to refer to the suggestions on pages 178-182 to help you locate and evaluate information and to write good paragraphs.

1. A period of trouble and dissatisfaction within a country can provide the opportunity for a leader to work his way to dictatorship.
2. If dictators are to accomplish their goals, they must find ways to squelch people's ability to think for themselves.

3. In a dictatorship, the government does not exist to serve the individual.

Evaluating Information

In your studies and in activities outside the classroom, you constantly need to evaluate information. To learn more about this skill, read the suggestions on pages 179 and 180. Then choose one of the following for a class project:

1. Cartoons about current events are commonly used to influence the thinking of the reader. As a class, study several cartoons from several different daily newspapers. Then discuss the following:
   a. What do the various symbols in the cartoons represent?
   b. Are the cartoonists trying to entertain, inform, or influence?
   c. Are the cartoons intended to appeal to the reader's emotions?
2. As a class, choose a topic and clip articles about it from various newspapers and news magazines. Study these articles carefully, and discuss the following questions:
   a. How do the headlines of each of these articles compare?
   b. Does each writer present the same facts?
   c. Does the writer interpret the story, and if so, how?

West Berlin is located deep inside East Germany. The Communists want to gain control of this area, but the free nations west of the Iron Curtain are determined to protect its liberty.

6 Berlin

A Study Guide

A Problem To Solve

West Berlin is so valuable to the United States and West Germany that they are willing to spend large sums of money each year to prevent Communist East Germany from taking it over. Why is West Berlin so important? In forming hypotheses, you will need to consider the following:

1. In what way was Berlin important before it was divided?

2. How was Berlin affected by World War II?

Terms To Understand

You need to know the following terms in order to read this chapter with understanding. Look up terms you do not know in the glossary of this book, a dictionary, or an encyclopedia.

Iron Curtain   sectors
Cold War   blockade

See TO THE STUDENT, pages 6-7.

Deep inside East Germany is the city of Berlin, Germany's prewar capital. Before World War II, Germany's leaders worked hard to make Berlin a great city. They laid out wide streets and large parks, and built beautiful public buildings, art galleries, theaters, and universities. Many factories were established in Berlin also. Berlin covers an area of 341 square miles. At the time World War II began, it had more than four million people.

World War II brought tragic changes to this splendid capital. Thousands of buildings were bombed, and more than a million people were killed or left the city. After the war, Berlin was divided. This chapter will explain why this division was made and will describe the two main sections of the city.

Berlin becomes a divided city. When Germany was divided by the Allies after World War II, the part of the country where Berlin is located was occupied by the Soviet Union. Berlin was too important to be taken over by one country alone, however. Therefore, the Allies agreed to treat it as though it were separated from the rest of Germany. They divided the city into four sectors, three

Soviet troops at the Brandenburg Gate in 1945. After Germany surrendered, Berlin was divided into American, British, French, and Soviet sectors. In the months that followed, the Western powers in Berlin found it increasingly hard to work with the Soviets.

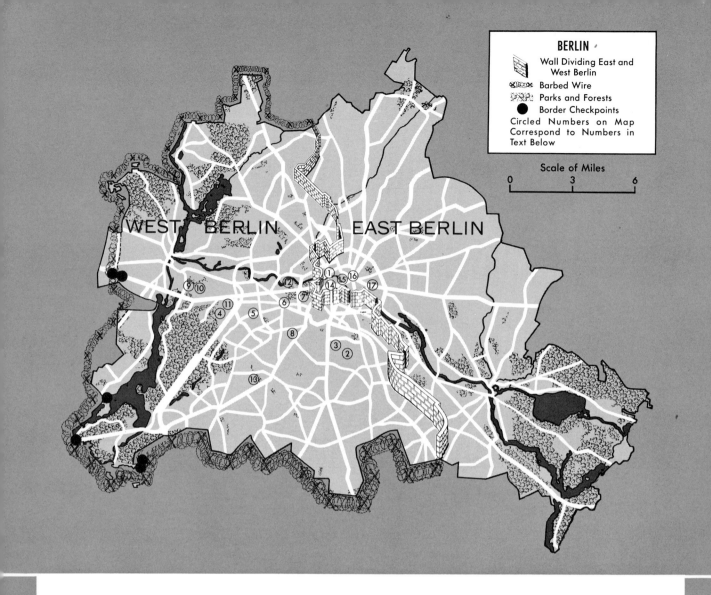

BERLIN
Wall Dividing East and West Berlin
Barbed Wire
Parks and Forests
Border Checkpoints
Circled Numbers on Map Correspond to Numbers in Text Below

Scale of Miles
0   3   6

WEST BERLIN

EAST BERLIN

PLACES OF INTEREST IN BERLIN

① **The Brandenburg Gate** is a huge archway with six giant columns, completed in 1791 under the rule of Frederick William II. Although it has long been a main gateway between eastern and western Berlin, the gate is now blocked by a wall built by the Communist government of East Germany.

② **Tempelhof Airport** is one of the largest and busiest airports in Europe.

③ **The Airlift Memorial** stands in memory of the men who died bringing supplies to the people of West Berlin during the Berlin Blockade.

④ **The Fairgrounds** is the site of many German and international exhibitions.

⑤ **The Kurfürstendamm** is the main boulevard in the shopping district of West Berlin.

⑥ **Kaiser Wilhelm Memorial Church** stands at one end of the Kurfürstendamm. It includes the ruins of a former church, to remind people of World War II.

⑦ **The Tiergarten** is a 630 acre park, one of the largest and most beautiful in Berlin. The Congress Hall, a modern building used for international meetings, is located in the park.

⑧ **Schöneberg Town Hall** is the meeting place of the West Berlin government.

⑨ **Waldbühne** (Forest Theater) is a large outdoor theater. Musical plays, variety shows, and displays of fireworks can be seen here during the summer.

⑩ **Olympic Stadium,** one of the largest sports grounds in Europe, was built for the

Olympic Games in 1936. It seats about 100,000 spectators.

⑪ **The Radio Tower** rises to a height of over 450 feet. Much of Berlin can be seen from this tower.

⑫ **The Hansa Quarter,** once an area devastated by the war, is now a district with new apartment houses, schools, and churches. These buildings were designed by architects from many nations.

⑬ **The Dahlem District** is a cultural center in West Berlin. At the Botanical Gardens, which are located here, trees and flowers from all over the world are displayed. In 1948 the Free University was established in the Dahlem District. Its founders were a group of students and professors who did not want to study under Communist domination at Humboldt University in East Berlin.

⑭ **Unter den Linden** is a boulevard in East Berlin. Its name means "under the linden trees." Unter den Linden was once Berlin's most splendid street, but suffered much destruction during World War II. After the war, rows of linden trees were replanted along the street, but the bombed out buildings were not rebuilt for many years. Recently, however, the Communists have worked to restore the boulevard to its former beauty.

⑮ **Marx-Engels Platz** is a city square in East Berlin where rallies and demonstrations are held.

⑯ **Alexander Platz** is a city square in East Berlin. The Berlin Town Hall, the meeting place of the East German government, is located here.

⑰ **Karl Marx Allee** is a main street in East Berlin. Many new buildings have been built along Karl Marx Allee to replace those destroyed in World War II.

The Brandenburg Gate has long been a main gateway between eastern and western Berlin. Now, however, it is blocked by the Berlin Wall, which was built by the East German government.

of which were occupied by the British, French, and Americans. The fourth sector, East Berlin, was occupied by the Soviets. The division of Berlin was supposed to be temporary. As soon as the Allies and the Germans signed a peace treaty, Germany was supposed to be reunited, with Berlin as its capital.

The Soviets try to gain control of Berlin. The first Allied soldiers to reach Berlin were the Soviets. Two months passed before other Allied troops came to the city. During this time, the Soviets appointed a group called the *Magistrat* to run the city. The *Magistrat* was largely controlled by German Communists who had been trained in the Soviet Union.

After the other Allies reached Berlin, a committee called the Allied *Kommandatura* Berlin was established to govern the city. This committee was made up of military officers from the United States, the Soviet Union, the United Kingdom, and France. The American, British, and French members of the *Kommandatura* felt that the *Magistrat,* which had been established by the Soviets, should be replaced by a government whose officials were elected by the people of Berlin. In 1946, a city-wide election was held in which the people of Berlin chose officials for a new city government. Very few of the government officials chosen in this election were Communists.

The election of 1946 showed the Soviets that it would be difficult for the Communists to gain control of Berlin as long as the people had the right to choose their own leaders. Britain, France, and the United States were determined to guard the democratic rights of the people in Berlin. The Soviet Union, however, was determined to destroy these rights, so the city could be brought under Communist control. As the months passed, it became more difficult for the Americans, British, and French to work with the Soviets in Berlin. Finally, in June of 1948, the Soviet member of the *Kommandatura* walked out of a meeting and refused to return.

The Berlin Blockade. The only way left for the Soviets to bring West Berlin under Communist rule was to drive the Americans, British, and French out of the city. Geography was on the side of the Soviets, for West Berlin was like a small island in East Germany. Supplies for the Western forces in West Berlin were brought in along roads, canals, railroads, and air routes that led through East Germany. Soon after the Soviet member of the *Kommandatura* walked out, however, all roads, railroads, and waterways to West Berlin were blocked. In addition to preventing the Allied forces from getting supplies, the blockade cut off supplies to the people of West Berlin. In this way the Soviets hoped to starve the West Berliners into giving in to Communist rule.

The Soviets overlooked two things in their planning — the courage of the people of West Berlin and the determination of the Western powers. There was one difficult, expensive, and dangerous way that supplies could still be brought in. This was by air. Day and night for nearly a year, heavily loaded airplanes flew into West Berlin, carrying coal, food, clothing, and many other needed supplies. At last, the Soviets were forced to realize that the Western powers and the West Berliners would not give up. In May, 1949, they agreed to lift the blockade. Supplies had to be

During the Berlin Blockade. In 1948, the Soviets tried to force the Americans, British, and French out of Berlin by closing all roads, railroads, and waterways that lead to West Berlin. The blockade failed, for the Western Allies brought in supplies by air.

brought in by air for several months longer, however, for the Soviets continued to interfere with land and water traffic to West Berlin. On September 30, the Berlin airlift finally ended.

Two governments are established in Berlin. During the blockade, other events took place in Berlin. In the summer, the Communists caused disturbances in the city lawmaking assembly, which met in the eastern part of the city. Finally, the assembly was forced to move to West Berlin. Then, in November, a new Communist *Magistrat* was formed to govern East Berlin. In this way, Berlin came to have two governments.

Berlin after the blockade. During the next eleven years, the Soviets became increasingly more irritated at having democratic West Berlin in the middle of Communist East Germany. This island of freedom was like a window into the Western world. East Germans who visited West Berlin saw people living in freedom and enjoying a high standard of living. (See pages 135 and 137.) This made them dissatisfied with life in East Germany.

It was easy for East Germans to escape through West Berlin to freedom. Thousands of East Germans had friends, relatives, or jobs in the western part of the city. If a person wanted to escape, he could go to West Berlin, pretending that he was going to work or for a visit. Once he was safely in West Berlin, the East German police could not harm

The Berlin Wall was built in 1961 by East Germany to prevent its people from escaping westward to freedom. Before the wall was built, almost three million East Germans had escaped through West Berlin to freedom. Many of them were young people or skilled workers.

him. From there, he could take a plane to West Germany. Between 1945 and 1961, almost three million East Germans escaped through West Berlin. Many of them were young people or skilled workers.

The Berlin Wall. The Soviets could not afford to lose so many people from East Germany, so they attempted to make it impossible for East Germans to get to West Berlin. On August 13, 1961, traffic between East and West Berlin was stopped. In the weeks that followed, a high wall was built between the two parts of the city. Anyone who was caught trying to cross it was shot on sight. By building the wall, the Communists openly admitted that they had

failed. The only way they could get most of the East Germans to live under communism was by turning East Germany into a giant prison.

A danger to world peace. The division of Berlin is one of the most serious threats to world peace. Nikita Khrushchev, former leader of the Soviet Union, called the presence of the Western powers in Berlin a "thorn." He demanded that they leave, and that Berlin become a "free city." The Soviet leaders who have followed Khrushchev feel the same way. Without protection, however, the people of West Berlin would almost certainly lose their freedom. The Western powers cannot risk letting this happen, for if the Communists succeed in taking over West Berlin, they will become bolder in trying to win other victories. Also, millions of people living in other Communist satellite countries will lose courage if the Communists are allowed to take over West Berlin. For these and other reasons, it might well mean the start of another world war if the Communists try to force the Western powers to leave West Berlin.

It is uncertain just how long Berlin will remain divided. In the meantime, the Western powers are trying to abide by the agreements they made with the Soviets at the end of World War II. The Allied *Kommandatura,* now made up only of French, American, and British representatives, still officially controls the city. In reality, however, it directs only the defense and foreign affairs of West Berlin. The people of West Berlin elect their own government officials. They also send representatives to the lawmaking assembly of West Germany, for according to the West German constitution, West Berlin is a *Land,* or state. However, these representatives are not allowed to vote, for West Berlin cannot assume its full responsibilities as a *Land* as long as the Allies abide by the agreements made after World War II. The Soviets no longer recognize these

John F. Kennedy in Berlin. The division of Berlin is one of the most serious threats to world peace. It might well mean the start of another world war if the Communists try to force the Western Allies to leave West Berlin.

The Kurfürstendamm is a wide boulevard lined with shops and sidewalk cafés, which leads through the heart of West Berlin's main shopping district.

agreements. They claim that Berlin is the capital of East Germany and cannot be treated as a separate unit.

A tour of West Berlin. The West German town of Helmstedt, at the border between East and West Germany, is the starting point for many tours going from West Germany to Berlin. Just beyond the town is a checkpoint, where East German policemen stamp passports and check baggage while Soviet soldiers look on.

A traveler driving to West Berlin passes many heavily loaded trucks on the highway. Those going toward the city are carrying food, or raw materials for factories. Those coming out of the city are transporting electrical articles, machinery, clothing, or other goods manufactured in West Berlin factories.

A certain amount of trade is carried on between East Germany and West

Berlin, but most of the supplies the West Berliners need are brought in from West Germany. West Berlin is able to pay for much of what it imports by selling its manufactured products. The West German government pays for the rest.

One of the first places visited by many tourists in West Berlin is the Kurfürstendamm, a wide boulevard that leads through the heart of West Berlin's main shopping district. New office buildings, restaurants, stores, and sidewalk cafés line the Kurfürstendamm. The windows of the stores are filled with fashionable clothing and modern appliances. At night, the sidewalks are brightly lit with neon signs and are crowded with people out for an evening's entertainment.

Located north of the Kurfürstendamm and near the border between East and West Berlin is the Tiergarten. This

The Tiergarten in West Berlin is a beautiful park covering 630 acres, which is located near the border between East and West Berlin.

park, which is 630 acres in size, was badly damaged during the war. New trees and shrubs have been planted here since then. There are many statues and monuments in the Tiergarten. Visitors to the park may also visit a zoo and attend outdoor concerts.

The Kurfürstendamm and the Tiergarten are only two of the many interesting places to visit in West Berlin. There is a chain of lakes where sailing boats can be rented. Also, there are museums and art galleries to tour.

Visitors in West Berlin find it hard to believe that this city was badly bombed during World War II. Factories, churches, and schools have been constructed since the war, and attractive new apartment buildings line many of the city's streets.

A tour of East Berlin. Travelers who wish to see East Berlin are usually able to take short bus tours into this part of the city. The people who visited East Berlin five years ago and return today are surprised at the changes they see. Most of the war rubble has been cleared away. Many new buildings have been constructed, although reconstruction has been less extensive here than in

Unter den Linden is one of East Berlin's most impressive streets. During the war, the rows of linden trees and the buildings that lined this street were heavily damaged. In recent years, the East German government has worked hard to restore Unter den Linden to its former beauty.

West Berlin. Some of the most impressive new buildings are located along Karl Marx Allee and Unter den Linden.

East Berlin still lacks the gaiety and sparkle of West Berlin, however. The new buildings in East Berlin have been constructed so poorly and cared for so badly that they look much older than they are. The cars and beautiful clothes displayed in the new stores along Unter den Linden are too expensive for most East Germans to buy, and are intended mainly for tourists. Some of the restaurants in East Berlin still offer good food, but in most the meals and service are poor. At night the streets of East Berlin are quiet except for the occasional barking of a dog.

Checking Your Understanding
1. How was Berlin divided after World War II?
2. What did the Soviets hope to accomplish when they blockaded Berlin in 1948 and 1949?
3. Why did the Soviets finally remove their blockade?
4. Why did the Communists build a wall between East and West Berlin?
5. Why is the division of Berlin a threat to world peace?
6. What are some ways in which the city of East Berlin differs from West Berlin?

Increasing Your Understanding
Imagine you have been sent to Berlin as a newspaper reporter. Choose one of the following events and write an article about it for your home newspaper:
1. the election of 1946
2. the beginning of the Berlin Blockade
3. the end of the Berlin Blockade
4. the halting of traffic between East and West Berlin — August 13, 1961

Before beginning your article, read about the event in this book and in other sources. The suggestions on pages 178-180 will help you to find and evaluate information. Remember that a good newspaper article always tells what, where, when, why, and how. The suggestions on pages 181 and 182 will help you write a clear, well-organized article.

Sharing Your Ideas
In recent history, Berlin has become one of the most important cities in the world. West Berlin is situated in Communist East Germany like an island of freedom. Think carefully about the following questions, and then prepare to discuss them as a class:
1. Can the people of West Berlin keep their freedom indefinitely? Give reasons for your answers.
2. How do Berlin and the wall that divides it represent the break between Communist and non-Communist nations?

Your discussion will be more successful if you use the suggestions on page 184.

Understanding History
Continue the time line of German history that you began in Chapter 3 by adding the important events mentioned in this chapter.

Thinking Creatively
The Berlin Wall represents a great tragedy in German history. The wall not only divides friends and families but it represents the division of the world's people into two opposing groups, Communist and non-Communist. Read about the Berlin Wall in this book and in other sources. The suggestions on pages 178-180 will be helpful to you in locating and evaluating information. Then choose one of the following projects:
1. Using the Berlin Wall as a subject, paint a picture, compose a poem, or write a descriptive paragraph.
2. In June of 1963, President John F. Kennedy visited the Berlin Wall and said, "The wall is an offense against history and humanity." Write an essay telling why the Berlin Wall is shameful to history and humanity.

Campaign posters in West Germany. West Germany's leaders are elected by the people and may be voted out of office if the people disapprove of their policies.

7 Government

A Study Guide

Thoughts To Help You

Every democracy has the following characteristics:

1. All of its people enjoy basic freedoms, such as freedom of speech, which are guaranteed by a constitution.
2. It has elections in which all candidates may campaign freely and citizens can vote by secret ballot for candidates they wish to represent them.
3. Its laws are made by elected representatives of the people, and the people have the power to vote these representatives out of office.
4. A majority of its people believe that democracy is good, and carry out their responsibilities as citizens of a democratic country.

As you study this chapter, compare the governments of East and West Germany, keeping in mind the characteristics of a democracy.

Terms To Understand

You need to know the following terms in order to read this chapter with understanding. Look up terms you do not know in a dictionary or an encyclopedia.

democracy	majority
constitution	citizens
candidates	ballot
campaign	representative

East Germany and West Germany have governments that are very different from each other. East Germany is a dictatorship, in which people must follow the orders of leaders they did not choose and cannot vote out of office. West Germany, on the other hand, is a democracy, and the people of West Germany have a real opportunity to decide how their government should be run. Each of the governments in divided Germany claims that the other is not the rightful ruling body of the people it governs.

Government in West Germany

Elections in West Germany. Elections in West Germany are much like those in the United States. Candidates of the different political parties campaign free- ly in the weeks before the election. On election day, voters register, then mark their ballots in private. All citizens twenty-one years of age or older may

Voters in West Germany mark their ballots in private. In addition to choosing their government representatives in free elections, the people of West Germany enjoy other rights, such as freedom of worship and freedom of speech.

Food-rationing procedures being carried out by American occupation forces after World War II. The Western Allies, who occupied the western part of Germany after the Nazis were defeated in 1945, helped the West Germans establish a democratic government.

vote. In most national elections, nearly nine tenths of the eligible voters take advantage of this privilege.

Democracy in West Germany. Choosing their government representatives in free elections is only one of the rights West Germans enjoy. Like the citizens of other democratic countries, the West German citizen may worship as he pleases and express his opinions freely in public. He may speak out against any law that he thinks is bad and work for its repeal. The police cannot force their way into his home without a court order. Among the other rights he enjoys is the freedom to work where he wishes and to change his job at will.

These rights and freedoms have not always been guaranteed to the German people. Throughout most of their history, these people have had little voice in their government. Before Germany was united, in the nineteenth century, Germans in different parts of the country were ruled by nobles, princes, or kings, who permitted little self-government. After the unification of Germany in 1871, the people continued to be ruled by leaders who opposed democracy. When Germany was defeated in World War I, a democratic government was established, but the Germans soon lost their freedoms to Adolf Hitler. (See Chapter 5.)

The defeat of Germany in 1945 left the country without a government. The Allies, whose military forces occupied Germany, took over temporary control. The Western Allies soon helped the people in the western part of Germany to establish democratic local and state governments.

The Western Allies had planned to work with the Soviets in forming a national government for all of Germany. When this became impossible, the Western Allies arranged for the state lawmaking assemblies to elect people to form a council, which would write a democratic constitution for West Germany. In 1949, a constitution called the Basic Law was approved by the Western Allied military leaders and adopted by the states. West Germans consider the Basic Law to be a temporary constitution, which will be used only until West and East Germany are reunited.

A democratic constitution alone is not enough to establish a democracy. Citizens must believe that democracy is the best form of government, and be willing to take the responsibility of governing themselves. Many West Germans have not yet developed this attitude. Although a large percentage of the people in West Germany vote at election time, few take interest in other government activities. If West Germany continues to develop peacefully, however, the West Germans may become a truly democratic people.

The Bundestag and Bundesrat. The two national lawmaking assemblies of West Germany are the Bundestag and the

Members of the Bundestag, one of West Germany's two national lawmaking assemblies. Bundestag members are elected directly by the West German people. West Germany's other national lawmaking assembly, the Bundesrat, consists of members appointed by the states.

Bundesrat, which meet in the *Bundeshaus* in Bonn. The Bundestag is similar to the House of Representatives in the United States. Its members are elected directly by the people. The members of the Bundesrat, however, are appointed by the state governments. One of the duties of the Bundesrat is to see that the rights of the individual states are respected by the federal government. The Bundesrat also helps to see that laws made by the federal government are carried out by the states.

Both the Bundesrat and the Bundestag study and vote on all federal laws that are made. Some bills, especially those that the state governments are in charge of carrying out, must have the approval of both assemblies before they can become law. Others can become law even if the Bundesrat votes not to approve them. The Bundestag can vote to pass these bills after the Bundesrat has voted against them.

The president and the chancellor. The head of state in West Germany is the president. However, the president of West Germany has little authority. His main duties consist of representing West Germany at various meetings and events, signing official papers, and performing other ceremonial acts. Like the members of the Bundesrat, the West German president is not elected directly by the people. Instead, he is elected for a five-year term by a group made up of the members of the Bundestag and of an equal number of representatives elected by the state governments.

The man who does the real work of running the West German government is the chancellor. He has the authority to establish government policy. The chancellor selects fifteen to twenty people to form a cabinet. Cabinet members are put in charge of different departments of the government, such as the Ministry of Health and the Ministry of Defense.

The chancellor is not elected directly by the people. He is nominated by the president and elected by the members of the Bundestag. The Bundestag also has the authority to vote the chancellor out of office. Before this is done, however, members must agree on a new chancellor. This rule helps to stabilize the government of West Germany.

Courts. In addition to the officials who run the government and make the laws, West Germany has judges who help to explain and enforce the country's laws. West German judges have the responsibility of making certain that people accused of crimes have fair trials. The judges also decide how people who are guilty of breaking the law should be punished.

West Germany has several different levels of courts where lawsuits may be tried and where people accused of crimes may be brought to trial. A person who feels that his trial at a lower court was unfair may appeal his case to the next higher court.

There are other types of courts in West Germany. One handles only law cases involving labor problems. There is also a special finance court and a court that deals with social security and public welfare problems. In addition, West Germany has a Federal Constitutional Court. This court has the power to decide whether or not the laws passed by the Bundestag and the Bundesrat are constitutional.

Germany Divided

All of the areas shown in shades of gray on the map above were part of Germany before World War II. Today, the easternmost areas, shown in the lightest shade of gray, are under Polish and Soviet administration. A comparison of this map with the map on page 120 shows that these territories are east of the Oder and Neisse rivers. The rest of the country is divided between the Federal Republic of Germany, commonly called West Germany, and the German Democratic Republic, commonly called East Germany. The city of Berlin is divided between East Germany and West Germany.

Germany became a divided country at the close of World War II. When the Allies met to discuss the future of Germany at the end of the war, the territories east of the Oder and Neisse rivers already had been occupied by the Poles and Soviets. The Western Allies agreed to let these territories temporarily remain under Polish and Soviet administration. The remainder of the country was then divided into four zones. France, Britain, the United States, and the Soviet Union each occupied one zone. Berlin was divided in a similar way.

The division of Germany and Berlin was intended to be temporary. Cold War disputes prevented reunification, however. The Western Allies, realizing that Germany could not recover as a fragmented nation, finally merged their three zones. The territory formerly occupied by these zones is now West Germany, a constitutional democracy with its capital at Bonn. The Soviet zone has become East Germany, a Communist dictatorship controlled by the Soviet Union. East Germany's capital is East Berlin.

The Soviets and the Poles say that the Germans no longer have any right to the territories east of the Oder and Neisse rivers. East Germany has given up all claim to these territories, but West Germany has not. Most of the Germans who lived in the eastern territories have moved to West Germany, however, and it is unlikely that the Soviets and Poles will give up these areas on terms acceptable to the West.

State and local government. According to the Basic Law, West Germany is a federal republic, made up of eleven states. One of these is West Berlin. (See page 77.) Each state, or *Land*, in West Germany has its own government and elected lawmaking assembly. Within the states are smaller divisions called *Kreise*, which are much like our counties. The *Kreise* as well as West German towns and cities have their own governments with elected officials.

Government in East Germany

Elections in East Germany. Elections in East Germany are very different from those in West Germany. Only one candidate is listed for each office on the ballot. If a voter is in favor of the candidates, he either checks the ballot or simply drops an unmarked ballot into the ballot box. A person wishing to vote against the candidates must write "no" on his ballot. He is not likely to do this because all voting is done openly.

East Germany goes from one dictatorship to another. A review of East Germany's recent history helps to explain

East Germans go through the formality of voting, but do not really choose their own leaders. Candidates must be approved by the SED, and only one name is listed for each office. Voters have little choice but to accept the SED-approved candidates, for all voting is done openly.

why elections are run in such a manner. When the Soviets first occupied eastern Germany, they believed that the people would willingly support the Communists. Consequently, in 1946 they allowed free local elections to be held. Not enough Communists were elected to gain control, however. As a result, the Soviets decided to use force to bring East Germany under Communist rule.

One of the first steps taken by the Soviets after the election of 1946 was to gain control of all political organizations in East Germany. The Social Democratic Party, the largest political party in East Germany, was forced to unite with the smaller, Communist Party. The new party formed by this union was called the Socialist Unity Party, or SED. It was controlled by Communists who took directions from the Soviet

Walter Ulbricht helped to found the German Communist Party. He is the dictator of East Germany, but his position depends on Soviet support.

Union and who received help and support from the Soviet military forces in East Germany. The Soviets also formed two new parties, called the Democratic Peasants' Party and the National Democratic Party, both of which were led by Communists and could be depended on to support the SED. To make it seem as though East Germany were a democracy, two non-Communist parties were allowed to continue operating. The strong leaders of these parties were removed, however.

Soon after the Western Allies began planning a government for West Germany, the Soviets organized a large meeting in East Germany called the German People's Congress. Delegates of different political parties came to the Congress. However, the Soviets made certain that most of them were members or supporters of SED. The German People's Congress first tried to persuade the West Germans not to form their own government. When it became clear that the West Germans intended to go ahead with their plans, the Congress chose four hundred people to form a council. Some of the council members were then appointed to work on a constitution. This constitution, which was adopted in 1949, closely resembles the constitution of the Soviet Union.

The East German constitution sounds democratic. It calls East Germany the German Democratic Republic, and provides for democratic institutions, such as elections for a lawmaking assembly. However, East Germany's government is actually a dictatorship run by the Communist-led SED. Most of the top leaders in the East German government also hold high offices in the SED and

The Volkskammer is East Germany's national lawmaking assembly. A majority of its members belong to the SED or to other Communist-controlled organizations. There is never any real debate in this assembly. Members always vote for the bills submitted by their Communist leaders.

merely use the government to carry out party policies.

The way elections are carried out in East Germany helps to explain how the Communist leaders stay in power. In all elections, the candidates must be approved by the SED. A majority of them must belong to this party or to other organizations that are Communist controlled. On election day, the people have little choice but to vote for these candidates. (See page 87.)

The Volkskammer. The lawmaking body of the East German government is the *Volkskammer*, whose members are elected in the manner already explained. This assembly meets only about eight times each year. According to the constitution, the political party with the most members in the *Volkskammer* chooses the minister president. This office is similar to the office of chancellor in the Federal Republic, but has much less power. The minister president and his cabinet inform the *Volkskammer* of the bills that the SED leaders want passed. There is never any real debate in the *Volkskammer* about these bills. They are supported with enthusiastic speeches and voted for by all members.

The Council of State. Many of East Germany's laws are made in the Council of State. This body was established as head of state in 1960 after the death of East Germany's first and only president. Walter Ulbricht, leader of SED, is presently head of the council. Resolutions made by this group have the force of law.

Courts. The leaders of East and West Germany have entirely different views on the purpose of courts and judges. Since East Germany is a Communist dictatorship, courts and judges are forced to carry out party policies. As a result, judges are controlled by the government and there are no checks on government power. Most judges are members of the SED and follow orders from party leaders. If a person is accused of working against the government, the courts are expected to find him guilty.

District and local government. Local government in East Germany is also controlled by the SED. East Germany is divided into fifteen districts. These are further divided into *Kreise*. The districts and *Kreise* as well as the cities have their own governments. All must obey orders from the central government. Walter Ulbricht, head of SED, has said, "When we push that little button, the last village must report back, within five minutes: Order executed."

Checking Your Understanding
1. What is the Basic Law?
2. How are the members of the Bundestag chosen? How are the members of the Bundesrat chosen?
3. What are the main functions of the Bundesrat?
4. How is the president of West Germany chosen? What are his main duties?
5. How is the chancellor of West Germany chosen?
6. What are some duties of judges in West Germany?
7. How do elections in East Germany differ from those in West Germany?
8. Why did the Communist government of East Germany discontinue free elections after 1946?
9. What is the SED? Why was it formed?
10. What is the *Volkskammer*?
11. How do the courts of East Germany differ from those in West Germany?

Making an Outline
Outlines can be very helpful both in writing reports and in understanding and studying what you have read. Using the suggestions on page 182, make an outline of this chapter. Use your outline to help you review the chapter when necessary.

Increasing Your Understanding
1. Write a report. Write a report comparing how a bill would pass through the West German government, the East German government, and the government of the United States. Use this book and other sources to find information. The suggestions on pages 178-182 will help you to find and evaluate information and to prepare a well-written report.
2. Make a chart. Make a chart showing the main governmental bodies of West Germany, East Germany, and the United States. List some of the main duties of each body on your chart. Refer to the suggestions on pages 178 and 179 to help you find information for your chart.

Ideas for Discussion
In our study of government, we often neglect to think of the basic purposes that government serves. As a class, prepare to discuss the following questions:
1. Why is government necessary?
2. What purposes does a government serve in a democracy?
3. What purposes does a government serve in a dictatorship?

Refer to the suggestions on page 184 to help make your discussion successful.

Part 3
A Divided Country at Work

Germany's leading mineral resources are coal, lignite, and potash. The Germans have built many steel and chemical plants to make use of these resources. They have also made good use of the resources nature has provided for farming, and have developed their rivers for transportation.

An industrial area in the Saar coalfields of West Germany

EAST GERMANY

WEST GERMANY

A chemical plant in the city of Halle, East Germany

An industrial area near Aachen, in West Germany. East and West Germany are among the world's leading producers of manufactured goods. West Germany is the leader of the two. It has a free economy and has received more foreign aid than East Germany.

8 Growth of Industry

A Study Guide

A Problem To Solve

Germany, now divided into East Germany and West Germany, is a leading industrial area. <u>How has the growth of industry in Germany been affected by geography and history?</u> In forming hypotheses, you will need to consider the following:

1. the natural resources of Germany
2. the attitudes and skills of Germany's people

3. the history of Germany
4. Germany's transportation system

Terms To Understand

You need to know the following terms in order to read this chapter with understanding. Look up terms you do not know in a dictionary or an encyclopedia.

natural resources	consumer goods
raw materials	synthetic

See TO THE STUDENT, pages 6-7.

Germany, now divided into East and West Germany, is a leading industrial area. West Germany produces more iron and steel than any country in Europe except the Soviet Union, and more automobiles than any country in the world except the United States. East Germany has a smaller industrial output than West Germany. Even so, it is the most important producer of manufactured goods among the Soviet Union's allies in Europe.

Long before it was divided, Germany was an important industrial nation.

The following paragraphs discuss how geography, history, and the type of people who live here helped to make it so.

How has geography influenced Germany's industrial growth? In the western part of Germany, nature placed one of the world's best coalfields and one of the world's best water highways close together. The waterway is the Rhine River, and the coalfield is in the Ruhr industrial district. Much of the coal in this district is the type that is needed for making steel. Iron ore and other raw

A combination of coal deposits and good transportation helped to make the Ruhr district of Germany one of the leading steel-producing areas in the world. Ruhr steel helped the Germans become important producers of machinery and other metal products.

materials also needed to make steel can be shipped to the Ruhr along the Rhine or along one of the canals that lead to this district. In addition, coal and manufactured goods from the Ruhr can be shipped to markets easily and cheaply. The combination of an important raw material and good transportation helped the Ruhr become one of the greatest industrial areas in the world. The steel made here helped Germany become one of the world's most important producers of machinery and other metal products.

Chapter 9 discusses other raw materials that affected the growth of German industry. There are large deposits of potash and other salts in Germany. Many chemical plants were built to make products such as fertilizer from these salts. The shortage of certain raw materials such as petroleum and iron

Learning to use machinery. Germany's highly skilled, hardworking people have made good use of the resources provided by nature.

ore also affected industry. In order to earn money to buy these raw materials from other countries, Germany needed to export manufactured goods. This need encouraged manufacturing to grow. Germany's fine railroads, waterways, and roads also affected manufacturing, for they made it easy for factories to obtain raw materials and send manufactured products to market.

How have Germany's people helped the growth of German industry? The gifts that the geography of a country provides are of no value unless the people make use of them. Fortunately, the Germans are a hardworking people who have made good use of their resources. As Chapter 17 helps to explain, German scientists and inventors have played an important part in developing Germany's industries. Also, the Germans have established excellent schools for training craftsmen and technicians. Without the skill and the will of her many people, Germany's vast industrial growth would not have been possible.

How has history influenced Germany's industrial growth? Historical events also have had an important effect on German industry. For a long period of time Germany was broken into many almost independent states. This discouraged the growth of industry. Each state demanded the payment of taxes, called tariffs, on goods brought across its borders from outside. The tariffs made it expensive to move raw materials and manufactured goods from place to place in Germany. The type of money used and the laws controlling business also differed from place to place. Therefore, few factories were built in Germany during the time that other countries,

Main Industries of Germany

The maps on this page show where four leading types of industries are located in East and West Germany. A comparison of these maps with the one on page 102 indicates that the location of some of these industries was determined by the availability of raw materials. For example, most West German steel plants are near coalfields, and many East German chemical plants are near deposits of potash. A good transportation system has made possible the establishment of many other types of industries throughout East and West Germany.

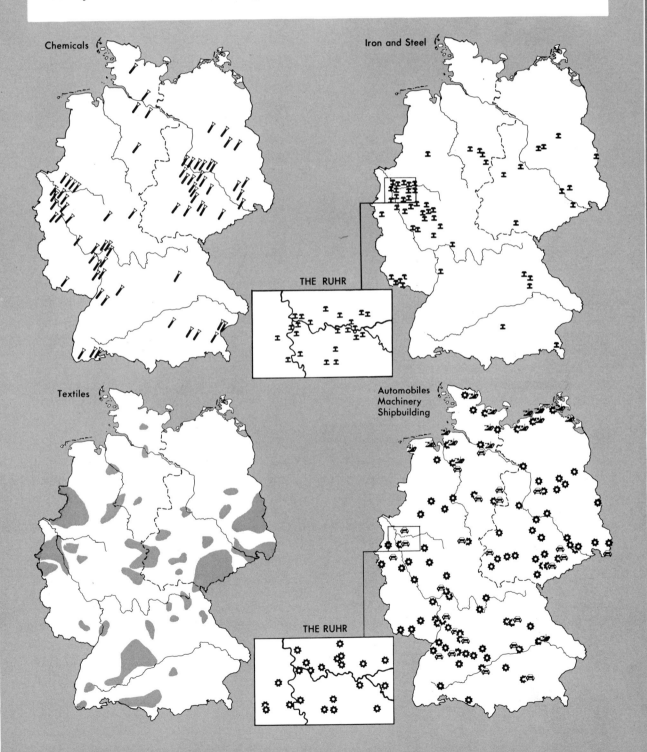

Chemicals

Iron and Steel

THE RUHR

Textiles

Automobiles
Machinery
Shipbuilding

THE RUHR

German industry was severely damaged during World War II. The United States has helped West Germany to rebuild and move ahead.

In one way, Germany was helped by the fact that its industries developed later than those of other countries. The Germans were able to make use of other people's experiences. They borrowed the best ideas about machinery and methods of manufacturing that had been developed in other countries and improved upon them. Within a relatively short time, Germany became one of the world's leading industrial nations.

During Hitler's rule, industry grew still more rapidly. Hitler wanted Germany to produce large quantities of airplanes, tanks, and weapons. To meet this demand, the iron and steel industry and the metal-products industries were greatly expanded. Hitler also wanted Germany to be as independent of other nations as possible. For this reason, large factories were built to produce synthetic rubber and gasoline. These artificial products largely replaced the natural rubber and petroleum that Germany had previously had to import.

After Germany was defeated in World War II, it seemed as though it would never again be a great industrial nation. Thousands of factories had been destroyed. Some factory buildings were still standing, but their equipment had been removed by Allied occupation forces as payment for the destruction Germany had caused during the war. In eastern Germany, especially, almost all industrial equipment that could be used had been removed.

Germany's future as an industrial nation looked dark for another reason. The Allies wanted Germany's military strength to be limited so that the Germans would not be able to start another war. The suggestion was even made that

such as Great Britain, were becoming industrialized. Instead, German craftsmen continued to make textiles or other goods in small workshops.

Many Germans realized that some form of cooperation was badly needed to overcome problems such as tariffs. About fifty years before Germany was united, Prussia and some of the other German territories agreed to exchange goods without charging each other tariffs. Out of this agreement grew a customs union called the Zollverein.* The Zollverein solved one of the problems that had made it difficult to start factories in Germany. After its establishment, industry began to grow. Industrial development increased more rapidly after Germany was united in 1871.

Germany be forced to become mainly an agricultural country. The Cold War has prevented the valuable skills of Germany's industrial workers from being wasted in this way, however. To learn how, let us look briefly at industry in West and East Germany since World War II.

Industry in West Germany

West Germany's industries are rebuilt. The Western Allied leaders rejected the idea that Germany be made into an agricultural country. They believed that the free world needed to be strong and prosperous in order to win the struggle against communism. The coal and steel of the Ruhr and the manufactured goods that the skilled West Germans could produce would add to this strength and prosperity. The Western Allies realized that West Germany would produce these goods willingly if it were treated as an equal partner.

The testing room of a compass plant in the port city of Kiel. There are many factories in the northern port cities of West Germany. Manufacturing cities are also located in the Ruhr, the Rhine Valley, and the rich central farmlands of West Germany.

The European Community

THE EUROPEAN COMMUNITY

① Netherlands   ④ Luxembourg

② Belgium   ⑤ France

③ West Germany   ⑥ Italy

What is the European Community? The map on this page shows six countries that are cooperating to increase trade with each other and to help their industries grow. These countries are cooperating through three organizations, called the European Coal and Steel Community, the Common Market, and the European Atomic Energy Community. The nations that belong to these three organizations are known as the European Community.

Why is the European Community needed? Through the centuries, national pride and rivalry have made cooperation between European nations very difficult. World War II forced the nations of western Europe to take a new look at the idea of cooperation, however. These nations had suffered terrible destruction during the war. Their economies had been greatly weakened, and their overseas colonies were demanding independence. In addition, they were threatened by the Soviet Union, which already controlled most of eastern Europe.

The countries of western Europe had to increase the amount of goods they manufactured before they could become strong and prosperous again. This was difficult to do, however, because they were small and faced with tariff barriers. (Tariffs are taxes that a nation places on goods coming in from outside its borders.) To see what a handicap this was, imagine what it would be like if each state of the United States were an independent country with high tariffs on imports. Manufacturers would have to pay more for raw materials imported from other states, because the cost of the tariff would be added to the price of these materials. The manufacturers also would have difficulty selling goods outside their states. The tariffs added to the regular price of products would make them too expensive for most people to buy. As a result, the manufacturers would have to sell mainly to people within the borders of their own states. With so few people to sell to, the manufacturers would not be able to earn enough to greatly increase their production.

The six countries shown on the map on this page decided to overcome their problems through cooperation. In 1952, the treaty establishing the European Coal and Steel Community went into effect. This organization gradually eliminated tariffs on coal, iron ore, scrap iron, and steel traded between member countries. In 1958, the Common Market came into being. This organization lowers tariffs and intends to eventually abolish them on all goods traded within the Community. It also permits workers to find jobs and businessmen to invest money in the industries of member countries. The third cooperative organization, the European Atomic Energy Community, was established in 1958. Through this organization, member nations develop peaceful uses for atomic energy.

What has cooperation accomplished? The European Community has become the world's largest trading power. In the six-year period following the establishment of the Common Market, industrial production in the member countries rose about 40 percent, and the standard of living rose more than 20 percent.

Cooperation has helped the member nations of the European Community in another way. It has established closer ties between countries that have often been enemies in the past. This cooperation may be the first of many steps toward a united Europe.

The United States gave West Germany a great deal of help, and the industrious West Germans used this aid well. In 1960, they produced nearly three times the manufactured goods that the entire country of Germany had produced in 1936. Today, West Germany is one of the leading industrial areas of the world.

The European Community. In addition to hard work and to help from the United States, there is another reason for West Germany's industrial growth. West Germany has cooperated with five neighboring countries in forming the European Community. (See opposite page.) As a member of the European Community, West Germany is able to obtain the raw materials needed by its factories and to sell its manufactured products more easily.

Industrial areas of West Germany. West Germany's main industrial district is the Ruhr, but goods are manufactured in many other areas. One important group of industrial cities is located in the Rhine Valley south of the Ruhr. There are also manufacturing cities in the rich central farmlands and along the North Sea coast. The map on page 95 shows some of the products that are manufactured in these and other areas.

Industry in a free country. An important part of West Germany's labor force is made up of refugees from East Germany who fled westward because they wanted to work in freedom and enjoy a higher standard of living. Factories in West Germany are owned by private individuals or companies and may manufacture whatever goods they feel they can sell. Many of them produce consumer goods such as clothing, furniture, and cars. As a result, there is an abundant supply of these goods for people to buy. More important than this kind of reward, however, is the freedom that West German workers enjoy. They are free to choose work they wish and to change jobs if they are dissatisfied.

Industry in East Germany

East Germany is a machine shop for the rest of the Communist world. The story of manufacturing in East Germany is similar to West Germany's in some ways, but different in others. The area that is now East Germany has no great coalfields and did not develop a great iron and steel industry before World War II. However, eastern Germany does have valuable deposits of potash and other salts. Before the war, chemical plants and other types of factories were built here to make use of these resources. Many skilled workers had jobs in these industries.

The Soviets, who gained control of eastern Germany after Hitler's defeat, realized the value of the supply of skilled labor here. Most of the Communist nations of the world were behind the free nations in manufacturing. German skilled workers could produce much of the factory equipment needed by other Communist nations.

The Soviets did two things to make factories in eastern Germany produce

East Germans produce machinery for other countries of the Communist bloc. All factories in East Germany are under government control, and produce what the government orders.

what was needed by countries in the Communist bloc. The Soviets arranged for the government to be taken over by German Communists who would follow Soviet orders. Then they had the government gain control of the industries. At first the government took over only the large factories. Gradually, the smaller ones were also taken over. Today, small workshops in East Germany are still owned by private individuals, but even these must follow government orders.

A department of the East German government, called the State Planning Commission, is in charge of industry. It plans the progress that industry in East Germany is to make and decides what each factory is to produce. Only

comparatively small quantities of clothing and other consumer goods may be manufactured, for the government wants East German factories to produce machinery and industrial equipment instead. The wages that workers receive and the number of hours they work each week are also decided by the government. People who are unhappy with their working conditions have difficulty changing jobs, for all jobs are controlled by the government.

East Germany is behind West Germany in manufacturing. East Germany's industries have grown since World War II, but they are still behind West Germany's. There are several reasons for this. The Soviets removed more equipment from East German factories than the Western Allies removed from western Germany after the war. Also, East Germany was required to make reparations* to the Soviet Union until 1954. In addition, the East Germans did not receive nearly as much outside help in rebuilding their war-torn industries as the West Germans.

The conditions under which East Germans must work also have held back the growth of industry in East Germany. For example, a man with an idea for a new product is not permitted to raise money and start a factory of his own. Also, workers in East Germany know that even if they work overtime to earn extra money, they probably will not be able to buy attractive clothing, cars, and other things they want, because these goods are very scarce. For these and other reasons, many East German workers have fled to West Germany. This loss of skilled labor has further hurt East Germany's industries.

Even though East Germany is behind West Germany, it is still an important producer of manufactured goods. No Communist nation except the Soviet Union exports as large an amount of machinery each year. This is one reason why the Soviet Union is determined to remain in control of East Germany.

Checking Your Understanding

1. How do East and West Germany compare with other countries in industrial production? Give specific examples.
2. How did geography help to make the Ruhr one of the leading steel-producing areas of the world?
3. How did Germany's transportation network help the growth of industry?
4. How have the German people helped the growth of industry?
5. Why did industry develop later in Germany than in some other countries, such as Great Britain?
6. How did the Zollverein help German industry grow?
7. Why did the Western Allies want West Germany to rebuild its industries after World War II?
8. In what ways has the European Community contributed to the industrial growth of West Germany?
9. What is the most important difference between factories in East Germany and factories in West Germany?
10. Give two reasons why East Germany is behind West Germany in manufacturing.

Increasing Your Understanding

Write a report comparing the European Community and the Zollverein. The following questions will help you as you think about information to include in your report:
1. What problems made it desirable to form each of these economic organizations?
2. What were some of the achievements of the Zollverein?
3. What are some of the achievements of the European Community?

You will want to use the information in this book and in other sources. The suggestions on pages 178 and 179 will help you find additional information. To help you organize your material into a well-written report you may want to refer to the suggestions on pages 181 and 182.

Keeping Up With the Times

The activities of the European Community organizations have an important effect on many countries throughout the world. Make a bulletin board display using newspaper and magazine clippings concerned with the affairs of any European Community organizations. As a class, discuss the most significant events reported in these clippings.

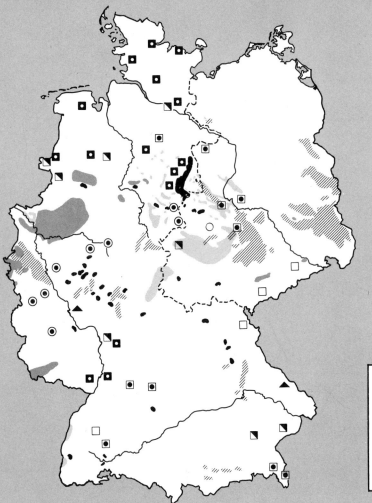

Coal, lignite, and potash are Germany's leading resources. Most of the coal deposits are in West Germany, and most of the lignite deposits are in East Germany. Both sections of Germany have deposits of potash. The potash deposits of Germany have enabled the Germans to become leading producers of chemicals, and the coal deposits have helped them to become leading producers of steel and of metal products.

German oil wells and iron ore mines do not produce as much oil and iron ore as are needed. Large quantities of these minerals are imported.

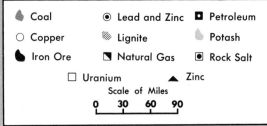

⬮ Coal	◉ Lead and Zinc	⬛ Petroleum
○ Copper	▨ Lignite	⬮ Potash
⬤ Iron Ore	◪ Natural Gas	▣ Rock Salt
☐ Uranium		▲ Zinc

Scale of Miles

0 30 60 90

9 Resources

A Study Guide

A Problem To Solve

The natural resources of a country help to shape its industrial development. <u>How have the natural resources of Germany affected German industry?</u> In forming hypotheses, you will need to think about how Germany's resources helped to determine the following:

1. the location of German industries
2. the type of industries developed by the Germans
3. the degree of industrial development achieved by the Germans

Chapters 8 and 10 contain additional information that will be useful in solving this problem.

See TO THE STUDENT, pages 6-7.

Germany as a whole is not rich in any natural resources except coal, lignite, and potash. In both East and West Germany, however, the people have made good use of the resources they do possess.

Coal and Lignite. Germany has large deposits of coal. Part of this is bituminous* coal, and part is a type of soft, brown coal called lignite. Most of the lignite is found in East Germany, and most of the bituminous coal is found in West Germany. The most outstanding bituminous coalfield in West Germany is in the Ruhr. Much of the bituminous coal mined here is suitable for making coke, the fuel which is used in smelting iron ore.

A smaller coalfield is located in the Saar.* The coal that is mined here must be mixed with higher-grade coking coal

*See glossary

Mine workers in the Ruhr. One of Europe's best coalfields is in West Germany's Ruhr district. Much of the coal here is suitable for coking.

USES OF COAL AND LIGNITE

One of the most valuable types of coal is that used for making coke, the fuel used in the smelting of iron ore. Much of West Germany's coal is suitable for coking. To make coke, coal is heated in large, airtight ovens until it becomes molten and the gases it contains bubble out. Then it is cooled until it forms hard, grayish-black lumps of coke.

The gas produced in the making of coke contains coal tar, ammonia, and other chemical compounds. This valuable gas is permitted to escape from the coking ovens through pipes. Then it is passed through tanks and pipes containing water. Here it goes through a cooling and washing process that removes much of the tar and other chemical compounds. More of these materials are removed by subsequent cleaning processes. The coal tar obtained in this manner is used in the manufacture of such products as dyes, medicines, motor fuels, plastics, and synthetic rubber.

Most of the world's coal is not suitable for coking. Non-coking coals are used as fuel in homes, factories, and electric power plants.

Lignite is one of the non-coking coals. It is a soft, brown coal that contains large amounts of moisture. When burned, it gives off less heat than other kinds of coal. German lignite beds generally lie close to the surface of the ground and are less expensive to mine than coal. As a result, factories and electric power plants near the lignite fields can obtain this fuel at a relatively low cost. Lignite is also used as a fuel for heating homes. In addition, chemists have discovered methods of making tar and synthetic gasoline from this raw material.

A lignite mine in West Germany. Germany has large deposits of lignite, a type of soft, brown coal. It is used as a fuel in homes, factories, and electric power plants.

in order to make good coke. Nevertheless, the Saar has become an important industrial area. This is partly because high-grade coking coal can be shipped easily by water from the Ruhr. Also, the Saar is located near an important iron-mining region in France.

Potash and rock salt. Some of the largest and most important potash beds in the world are found in Germany. As the map on page 102 indicates, both East and West Germany are endowed with deposits of this mineral. Potash is used in the manufacture of fertilizer. It is also used in making glass, soap, and explosives.

Germany has large deposits of rock salt. Some of these are found underneath the potash beds. Salt is used in

making a number of chemical products, such as chlorine and bicarbonate of soda.

Other minerals. The map on page 102 shows that Germany has deposits of a number of other minerals. West Germany is one of Europe's main producers of petroleum. Both East and West Germany also have iron ore deposits. Neither division of Germany produces enough of either mineral to meet its needs, however. West Germany imports about half the iron ore used by its iron and steel industry, and an even larger proportion of its petroleum. East Germany must also import large quantities of these two important minerals.

Forests. Dense forests cover about one fourth of the land in Germany.

Many trees have been planted on land that is unsuited to crops. Trained foresters select the types of trees that will grow well in each kind of soil. They decide how dense the forests should be and when the trees should be cut. When trees are cut, new seedlings are planted in their places. Through conservation, the Germans are able to produce a large part of the wood needed in their woodworking industries and paper mills.

Rivers. The rivers of Germany are another important resource. Many hydroelectric* dams have been built on the swiftly flowing rivers in central and southern Germany. Besides being a source of power, Germany's rivers are used for transportation. (See Chapter 12.)

A sawmill in the Black Forest. About one fourth of the land in Germany is forested. The Germans take excellent care of their forests.

Increasing Your Understanding

Choose two of the topic sentences listed below and write a paragraph for each. In each paragraph, expand and explain the idea in the topic sentence, using information in this book.

1. Coal that can be used to make coke is one of West Germany's most valuable minerals.
2. Germany has valuable resources in addition to coal.
3. The Germans have made good use of the resources they possess.

Learning More About the Ruhr

The Ruhr district of West Germany is one of the world's leading industrial areas. It has also played an important part in German history. To learn more about the Ruhr, write a report. Try to answer the following questions in your report:

1. Where is the Ruhr district located?
2. Why is this district important to German industry?
3. What effect did World War II have on the Ruhr industrial district?
4. What part did the Ruhr play in the formation of the European Coal and Steel Community?

The suggestions on pages 178-182 will help you find and evaluate information and organize your material into a well-written report.

Finding More Information

The people of Germany have made good use of their mineral resources. Learn more about these resources and their uses by making a mineral chart. Organize your chart so that an observer can easily find:

1. a brief description of each mineral
2. where deposits of the mineral are located in Germany
3. how the mineral is mined
4. some main uses of the mineral

(Include all the minerals listed in the key box on page 102.) Use samples and illustrations wherever possible. You will need to do research in this book and other sources. The suggestions on pages 178 and 179 will help you find additional sources.

West Germany is a leading producer of automobiles. In order to import food and raw materials it needs, West Germany must export large quantities of manufactured goods.

10 Products of Industry

A Study Guide

Thoughts To Help You

Generally, there are good reasons why a country has certain types of industries. In your study of this chapter, look for the following:

1. reasons why West Germany is a leading producer of iron and steel
2. reasons why both East and West Germany are important producers of chemicals
3. reasons why industries that depend on agricultural raw materials are not very important in West Germany
4. the reason why East Germany's iron and steel industry has been greatly expanded since World War II

West Germany must import large quantities of raw materials and food. In return, it exports products made in West German factories. Without this exchange of manufactured goods for raw materials and food, the people of West Germany would not enjoy such a high standard* of living.

*See glossary

Iron and steel. The blast furnaces and the steel plants of West Germany produce more iron and steel than those of any country in Europe except the Soviet Union. Most of the steel plants are located near the Ruhr coalfields. (See maps on pages 95 and 102.)

Metal products. Steel made in the Ruhr and other parts of West Germany is used in making many different types of metal products. The map on page 95 shows where some of these metal products are manufactured. Scattered throughout West Germany are automobile plants. In the northern port cities are shipyards. West Germany is a leading producer of both cars and ships.

West Germany is also one of the world's leading producers of machinery and machinery parts. Among the most valuable types of machinery made here are machine tools. These are power-driven tools that cut, grind, or bore holes through metal to make parts used in manufacturing other machines. Metal parts for machinery, such as bolts, springs, and locks, are also manufactured in West Germany.

Chemicals. West Germany is also a world leader in the manufacture of chemicals. This is due partly to its large reserves of coal, potash, and rock salt. Discoveries made by German scientists in the field of chemistry have also helped the German chemical industry to grow. Among the products made from coal tar in West Germany are dyes, medicines, and synthetic rubber. Other products of the West German chemical industry are fertilizers and synthetic fibers.

Textiles. The manufacture of textiles is another important industry in West Germany. Cotton, wool, and other raw materials are spun into yarns and threads, and these are woven into beautiful fabrics. With the exception of those used to make synthetic fabrics, almost all the raw materials for West Germany's textile industry must be imported. A large amount of cotton is purchased from the United States. Wool is imported from Argentina and Australia. West Germany's large population provides a good market for textiles, but some textiles are also exported.

Other products of industry. The German people excel in making articles that require skill to produce. German cameras, field glasses, optical lenses, scientific instruments, and watches are among the finest in the world. Electrical equipment, such as dictating machines and radios, are also made in

Textiles are manufactured in many parts of Germany. Most of the raw materials used by German textile mills are imported.

West Germany. In addition, West Germany has skilled craftsmen who make fragile articles of porcelain and glass. The delicately carved clocks, toys, and musical instruments of West Germany are also world famous. Many small toy factories and wood-carving shops are found in the Black Forest and Bavaria, in the southern highlands.

Most of the farmland in West Germany is used to produce food for the people rather than raw materials for industry. There are, however, some smaller industries that use farm products as raw materials. Sugar beets are processed to make sugar. Cattle hides are used to make leather products such as shoes. World-famous wines are made from grapes grown in the southern valleys, and hops raised in Bavaria are used in making beer.

A wood-carver in the Black Forest. The Germans excel in skilled craftsmanship.

An East German iron foundry. Before World War II, eastern Germany obtained most of the steel it needed from western Germany. Since the war, East Germany has expanded its iron and steel industry.

Products of East German industry. The map on page 95 shows that East Germany produces the same types of manufactured goods as West Germany. The chemical industry has long been important here, for there are large supplies of potash and other salts in this part of Germany. Machinery and optical goods are among the other products manufactured in East Germany. As Chapter 8 discusses, factories here supply much of the machinery used by other Communist countries.

Before World War II, metal-product factories in eastern Germany obtained most of the steel they needed from western Germany. A large steel industry had not developed in eastern Germany, partly because this part of the country had no large deposits of bituminous* coal like those in the Ruhr. Since the division of Germany, East Germany's steel industry has been greatly expanded. Raw materials for East Germany's steel industry are brought in from other Communist countries.

Checking Your Understanding

1. Why is the export of manufactured products important to West Germany?
2. In West Germany, what important industries depend on steel?
3. What industries in West Germany use farm products?
4. What are some reasons why West Germany has become a world leader in the manufacture of chemicals?

Sharing Your Knowledge

The iron and steel industry helped to make Germany an industrial power. As a class, make a study of the iron and steel industry. First of all, you may want to divide into committees. Each committee can then study one of the following:

1. the importance of steel in the modern world
2. the raw materials that are needed in making iron
3. how iron is made in a blast furnace
4. how iron is changed into steel
5. the different types of steel and their uses

The suggestions on pages 178 and 179 will help you locate information. Each committee may want to report the results of its study to the rest of the class. Reports will be more interesting if charts and pictures are used. Refer to pages 181-184 for suggestions to organize your information and to work together successfully.

A Class Trip

Plan a class visit to an iron or steel plant, a chemical plant, or other important industry in your community or nearby. Before the trip, you may want to do some reading about the type of industry you plan to visit. The suggestions on pages 178-180 will help you to find and evaluate information. After your trip, write a report. Tell what materials and processes were used to make the goods you saw produced. The suggestions on pages 181 and 182 will help you write a good report.

Finding More Information

German scientists and inventors have made important contributions to the development of industry. Choose one of the following scientists or inventors and write a report about him. Tell how his inventions or discoveries contributed to the growth of German industry. The suggestions on pages 178-182 will help you locate and evaluate information and organize your material into a well-written report.

Gottlieb Daimler
Wilhelm Maybach
Werner von Siemens
Karl Benz
Justus von Liebig
Fritz Haber
Adolf von Baeyer

Fields in the Saar region of West Germany. West Germany has a large population and relatively little land suited by nature to farming. However, the West Germans are able to supply about two thirds of their own food needs.

11 Farming

A Study Guide

Thoughts To Help You

One of the most important problems every nation must solve is obtaining the food its people need. As you read this chapter, find out:

1. how the West Germans are able to provide such a large proportion of West Germany's food needs

2. why the size of farms in West Germany creates serious problems

3. why East Germany does not raise enough food

Farming in West Germany

The farmers of West Germany supply about two thirds of their country's food needs. This is an amazing achievement when you remember that West Germany is densely populated and has relatively little land that is suited by nature to farming.

The farmland of West Germany. Much of the land in West Germany had to be improved before it could be used for agriculture. Today, about two thirds of the entire area of West Germany is farmland, used either for raising crops or grazing livestock. This farmland may be divided into three main regions. The first is the northern lowland farming region, the second is the central farming region, and the third consists of the farmland in the southern highlands.

Farmland of the northern lowland. Much of the northern lowland farming region was once considered unsuitable for farming. The soil here is generally poor and was formerly covered with swamps and marshes. Some land along the North Sea coast used to be under the sea. The industrious Germans, however, have overcome these problems in many parts of the lowland. In some areas, marshland has been drained and

In northern Germany, much land once unsuited to farming is now being farmed. The Germans have drained marshes and improved the land in other ways.

In central Germany there are areas of very fertile soil called loess.* Some of Germany's best farmlands are located in this part of the country. Houses in the farm villages here are built close together as though to leave as much land as possible for crops.

reclaimed, and is now used for grass-land. In the northwestern coastal area dikes protect land reclaimed from the sea. Farmers in the north are able to raise such crops as rye, oats, and potatoes. Today, farming is the most important occupation in the northern lowland.

The central farming region. Some of Germany's best farmland is in the central farming region. It stretches east and west along the southern edge of the lowland, and contains areas of very fertile soil called loess.* In the central farming region are large, prosperous villages where farmers have built their houses close together, as if to leave as much land as possible for growing crops. Woodlands have been cleared and crops grow to the edge of the roads.

Farming in the southern highlands. In the southern highlands, there is valuable farmland in the valleys of the Rhine River and its branches. Some farming is done on the hillsides and mountain slopes. In the valleys, the soil is very fertile and the summers are long and warm. On the steeper hillsides the land is not so suitable for growing crops. However, many steep slopes have been terraced, and land has been cleared so that grapes and other crops can be grown. In the highest parts of this region, much of the land is poor and stony, and there are many forests. Winters here are long and cold. Since most crops cannot be cultivated in these high areas, the land is used for grazing livestock.

112

*See glossary

West Germany's main farm products. Livestock raising has increased in importance since the end of World War II. Dairy cows and pigs are the main farm animals. Livestock is raised throughout the country, but is especially important in the northern lowland. Much of the land here that is not good for crops can be used to grow grass for grazing livestock. Raising livestock is also important in the highland region, for slopes that are too steep and infertile for farming can often be used for grazing.

German farmers have learned what crops are best suited to each of their main farming regions. They have found that some crops grow best in certain types of soil and climate that are found in only a few parts of the country.

More than half the cropland in West Germany is used for growing grain. Oats and rye are raised throughout the country, but are particularly suited to the poor soil and damp climate of the northern lowland. Wheat, which needs better soil and a drier climate, is the main grain crop in the central farmlands and the fertile southern valleys. Much of the wheat and rye is used to make flour. Oats are used mainly as animal feed.

Sugar beets and potatoes are other important crops in West Germany. After sugar beets are processed to make sugar,

A farm woman in West Germany. Many West German farms are too small to be efficient and to provide a good living for the families who work them.

the remaining beet pulp is used as feed for livestock. Potatoes are also used as food for livestock, as well as being an important food for people. In addition, potatoes are used to make alcohol and starch.

In the warm, sunny valleys of the southern highlands, grapes, tobacco, and hops are important crops. Hop flowers are used to flavor beer, and grapes are used to make wine. Apples, pears, and cherries are also grown here in abundance.

The farmers of West Germany obtain high crop yields. The harvest per acre of land in West Germany is larger than in Italy or France. This is partly because West German farmers work hard to improve and conserve their soil. They use large amounts of fertilizers to enrich poor soil. German farmers also have practiced crop rotation for many years. For example, in parts of Germany, fields are planted in wheat one year, sugar beets the next year, and barley the following year. Crop rotation helps to prevent the soil from becoming worn out.

The growing use of farm machinery in West Germany also helps to explain why crop yields are high. The number of tractors, combines, and other types of farm machines has increased greatly. In addition to making it possible to produce more food per acre, the increased use of farm machines is making it possible for a smaller number of farmers to supply food for a greater number of people.

West German farm problems. In spite of the high crop yields obtained by West German farmers, agriculture in West Germany faces problems. The most serious problem is the fact that most of the farms in West Germany are too small to be efficient and to provide a good living for farmers and their families. The average size of a West German farm is about twenty acres, while in the United States the average-size farm is about three hundred acres. Some West German farmers work at other jobs to add to their farming income. Many farmers are not able to earn enough money to buy a tractor or other farm equipment to help increase their productivity. As a result, the average West German farm worker produces much less than the average farm worker on a United States farm.

To help farmers earn incomes like those earned by other workers, the German government has established a system of farm subsidies.* This system has caused additional problems, however. It has encouraged many of the smallest, most inefficient farmers to continue to farm. Partly because of this inefficiency, West Germany's agricultural products are more expensive than the same farm products in other countries of the European Economic Community, or Common Market. (This organization is discussed on page 98.) Consequently, the West German farmers are not able to compete with the farmers in other Common Market countries.

The West German government has been aware for some time of these farm problems. In an effort to solve them, the Agricultural Law was passed in 1955. In accordance with this law, a detailed report on the state of agriculture is made to the Bundestag* each year. This report, called the Green Report, is accompanied by a Green Plan, which

Farm machines are becoming much more common in West Germany. The use of farm machinery is making it possible for a smaller number of farmers to supply food for a larger number of people.

outlines what will be done to solve agricultural problems.

One chief objective of the Green Plans is to increase the size of farms. Through the Green Plans, low-interest loans are made available to farmers who wish to enlarge their farms. Many farmers are buying or leasing land from farmers who are leaving their farms to work in industry. In this way, small farms are being joined together to form larger, more efficient ones. The Green Reports have shown, however, that farms are growing much too slowly.

Many farmers continue to divide up their farmland among their children, just as their fathers and grandfathers always did.

In addition to lending money to farmers who want to enlarge their farms, the Green Plans provide loans to farmers who wish to buy more farm machinery and to build new farm buildings. Agricultural research and training are encouraged, and an advisory service for farmers is maintained by the Green Plans. These measures will help to improve agricultural productivity.

115

Farming in East Germany

Farming in East Germany is like farming in West Germany in some ways, but in other ways it is very different. The land and climate of the two parts of Germany are on the whole quite similar, and most of the same crops are raised. East Germany does not have as many vineyards, however.

The main differences between farming in the two parts of Germany are in the size of farms and the way they are run. Before World War II, western Germany was important mainly as a manufacturing area. The farmland here was divided into small farms that were usually owned by the men who worked them. Although these men farmed their land carefully, western Germany still had to import much of its food. Eastern Germany, however, was more important as a farming area. Much of the farmland here was on large estates that were

A potato-harvesting machine in East Germany. East German farmers raise most of the same crops as West German farmers, for the two parts of Germany have similar land and climate. In East Germany, however, all farming is collectivized.*

cultivated by hired workers. Farmers in eastern Germany produced more food than they needed and sent the extra farm products to other parts of the country.

After the Communists took over the eastern part of Germany, they made important changes in farming. All estates and farms in East Germany that were more than 247 acres in size were taken over by the East German government. The government kept some of these and divided others among farmers who had little or no land. Then the government began to encourage farmers to join their small farms together to form agricultural-producers' cooperatives.* These were required to deliver part of their harvest to the government at a low price.

Many East German farmers did not want to join agricultural-producers' cooperatives, but they had little choice. For one reason, individual farmers were forced to deliver a part of their harvest to the government at an even lower price than the cooperatives received. Individual farmers also had to pay higher prices for fertilizer and equipment. In these and other ways, the government made life very difficult for those who tried to keep their own farms. By 1960, farming in East Germany had been completely collectivized.*

Collectivization has brought hardship to East Germany. Thousands of farmers have fled to West Germany. The farmers who remain produce less food per acre than West German farmers do, even though more farm machinery is used in East Germany. Today, East Germany, once able to export farm products, does not produce enough food for its people.

Checking Your Understanding
1. West German farmers provide about two thirds of their country's food needs. Why is this an amazing achievement?
2. The northern lowland was once considered unsuitable for farming. How has it become one of West Germany's important farming areas?
3. Where is the best farmland in the southern highlands located?

Learning More About Farming in Germany
Make a map. Make a map of Germany showing where different crops are grown. You may want to trace one of the maps in this book. Be sure your map has a key box that shows what each symbol on your map represents. (See page 174.) Attach the symbols in appropriate locations on your map. Your key box should include a title for the map. Write a report. When you have finished your map, write a report about the effect of Germany's land and climate on farming. Use this book and other sources to help you locate information. The suggestions on pages 178-182 will help you to find and evaluate information and to organize your material into a well-written report.

Interpreting Pictures
Pictures are an important source of information, particularly in the study of geography. Study the photograph on page 110, and answer the following questions:

1. What does the picture tell you about the land features in this area of Germany?
2. What does it tell you about the use of land?
3. What "educated guesses," or hypotheses, can you make about the land from this picture?

Discuss these questions with your class. Refer to the suggestions on page 184 to help you have a good discussion.

The Mittelland Canal crossing the Weser River. To expand their water transportation facilities, the Germans have deepened rivers and built hundreds of miles of canals. Germany's network of waterways makes it possible to transport bulky goods easily and inexpensively.

12 Rivers and Canals

A Study Guide

Thoughts To Help You

Germany has a number of rivers. Using these as a foundation, the Germans have created a fine system of water transportation. As you study this chapter, see how water transportation in Germany has been affected by each of the following:
1. the natural waterways of Germany
2. Germany's location in Europe
3. the division of Germany

Since early times, the waterways of Germany have been used as highways by people. Thousands of years ago, Germanic tribesmen traveled along these rivers through a wild, untamed land, carrying furs, leather, and amber.

Today, water travel is still an important means of transportation within both East and West Germany. However, boats are permitted to travel between these two areas on only a few of the waterways that connect them.

The Rhine River. Germany's most heavily traveled river is the Rhine, in West Germany. This great waterway rises in the mountains of neighboring Switzerland and empties into the North Sea. Ships from many nations travel along the Rhine River, for it is Europe's leading water highway. Many of these ships carry goods to and from the important industrial district of the Ruhr, in West Germany. The important industrial city of Duisburg, located where the Ruhr River meets the Rhine, is one of the largest river ports in Europe.

South of the Ruhr district, the smoky industrial cities along the Rhine give way to quiet towns, and the smoking chimneys of chemical and steel plants are replaced by thick forests, green vineyards, and ancient castles. The peaceful beauty of the countryside along the Rhine attracts thousands of travelers each year. Because of its unusual beauty, this beloved river has gained fame in German folklore and song.

Other waterways of Germany. Boats and barges travel over many other waterways in Germany. River channels

The Rhine River is Germany's most heavily traveled waterway. It begins in the mountains of Switzerland and empties into the North Sea. The Rhine is used by ships of many countries.

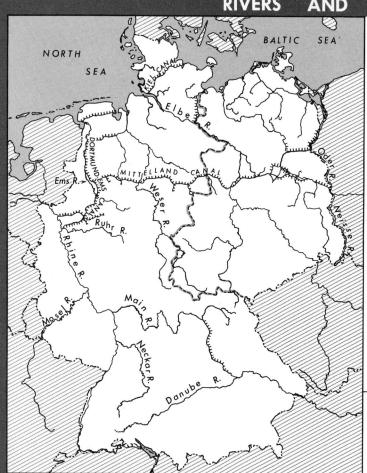

The rivers of Germany have long been used as water highways by people. Today in East and West Germany, water transportation is still important. Ships are permitted to travel between these two areas along only a few of their connecting waterways, however.

Germany's leading waterway is the Rhine River, which begins in Switzerland and empties into the North Sea. The Rhine is the most heavily traveled water highway in Europe and is used by ships from many nations.

Canals have been constructed to link many of Germany's rivers. Among these is the Dortmund-Ems Canal, which connects the Ruhr industrial district and the North Sea port of Emden. The canals and rivers of Germany are used mainly for transporting bulky freight, but they also carry some passenger traffic.

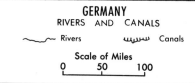

GERMANY
RIVERS AND CANALS

∿∿ Rivers   ⌣⌣⌣ Canals

Scale of Miles
0   50   100

have been made deeper, and hundreds of miles of canals have been constructed. One of the most important of these man-made waterways is the Dortmund-Ems Canal in West Germany. This forms an important link between the Ruhr industrial district and the North Sea port of Emden. The Mittelland Canal is important also, for it connects many rivers in the northern lowlands. In the far north, ships sail between the North and Baltic seas along the Kiel Canal.

Germany's network of waterways makes it possible to transport bulky products easily and cheaply. Ocean vessels from other parts of the world dock at the port cities of Germany. Some carry raw materials, such as iron ore.

Others bring grain, meat, machinery, or wood products. Riverboats and barges carry these products inland, and return to the coast carrying manufactured goods and other products from the interior.

Main seaports of Germany. West Germany's main seaports are Hamburg and Bremen. Both of these ports handle traffic coming and going from the North Sea. However, neither port is located on the coast. Hamburg is located on the Elbe River where ocean traffic and inland water traffic meet. Bremen is located about forty miles inland on the Weser River. Much of its oceangoing traffic is handled by its advance port of Bremerhaven. (See map on page 140.)

Hamburg is much larger than Bremen. It has miles of piers and railroads, and many blocks of warehouses and offices. Canals crisscross the city, and railroads and highways reach all the docks. Ships from nearly every country come to this port. (See picture on page 142.)

The Baltic ports of West Germany are less important than Hamburg and Bremen. There are several reasons for this. The North Sea seldom freezes in winter as the Baltic does. Therefore, ships can sail in and out of the North Sea harbors all winter long. Also, the North Sea is closer to the heavily traveled North Atlantic shipping route, which leads between Europe and North America. Another reason why the Baltic Sea ports of West Germany are less important is that they formerly carried on most of their trade with the eastern part of Germany and with countries in eastern Europe. Since these countries have been taken over by Communists, they trade less with West Germany, so fewer ships now come to the ports on the Baltic coast.

East Germany, which borders on the Baltic Sea, does not have any ports as large as Hamburg or Bremen. However, the East Germans are developing the port of Rostock. (See map on page 140.)

Checking Your Understanding

1. In what ways is water transportation important to West German industry?
2. Why are the ports of Hamburg and Bremen more important than West German ports along the Baltic Sea?
3. Describe several scenes you might see while traveling down the Rhine.

Learning From Maps

Maps can often help us understand important relationships between transportation, natural resources, and the location of industry. Compare the maps on pages 95, 102, and 120, and as a class discuss the ways in which the following rivers and canals influenced the development of German industry. You may want to refer to the suggestions on page 184 before beginning your discussion.

Kiel Canal   Danube River
Mittelland Canal   Elbe River
Dortmund-Ems Canal   Rhine River

Finding More Information

Many German legends and myths are connected with the Rhine River. To find out more about Rhine folklore, choose one of the following projects:

1. Read about the Lorelei in an encyclopedia. Also read a translation of the poem "The Lorelei" by Heinrich Heine. Write a brief report summarizing the myth of the Lorelei. You may want to use quotations from Heine's poem in your report.
2. Read about the Mouse Tower in *Grimm's Fairy Tales* and in other sources. Write a brief report on the legend of the Mouse Tower.
3. Read about nixes, and write a description of the folklore surrounding these water elves.

The suggestions on pages 178-182 will be helpful in locating and evaluating information and in writing your report.

Increasing Your Understanding

It is important to understand the many uses of rivers since they are so significant to mankind. Write a report about rivers answering the questions listed below. Use the information in this book and in other books for your report. The suggestions on pages 178 and 179 will help you locate other sources.

1. How is a river formed?
2. What is the difference between the upper, the middle, and the lower course of a river?
3. Why are rivers so important to man?

Superhighways called autobahns were first built in Germany during the 1930's. Since World War II, West Germany has greatly expanded its highway system. Good transportation has helped West Germany become a leading producer of manufactured goods.

13 Transportation and Communication

A Study Guide

Thoughts To Help You

The countries in our modern world that are prosperous and strong have good transportation systems. As you study this chapter answer the following questions:

1. How do Germany's transportation facilities compare with those of other parts of the world?

2. What part has good transportation played in the development of German industry?

3. What effect has the division of Germany had on the free movement of goods and people throughout this divided country?

Travelers may journey through West Germany by air, land, or water. Pleasure steamers on the Rhine River carry them past wooded hills and ancient towns. Modern trains speed them across the countryside, past large cities and pleasant little villages. People may also travel by automobile or bus over modern, four-lane highways. They may cross West Germany in less than an hour by airplane, or they may choose to bicycle slowly along country roads.

West Germany's excellent transportation system makes it easy to transport freight from one area to another. This has helped West Germany to become one of the world's leading producers of manufactured goods. (See Chapter 8.)

Waterways in West Germany. The map on page 120 shows the network of rivers and canals that stretches through the plains and valleys of West Germany. These waterways are used mainly by riverboats and barges, which carry manufactured goods to market, or move coal and other raw materials from mines to smelters and factories. There is also a good deal of passenger travel on West Germany's waterways.

West Germany's railroads. There are many more miles of railroads than waterways in West Germany. Like the waterways, these railroads carry raw materials and manufactured products to all parts of West Germany, as well as to other parts of Europe. Most of the railroads are government owned.

Train travel in West Germany is very pleasant. The trains are spotlessly clean, and arrive and depart on schedule. All express trains have modern dining cars. Trains traveling to distant cities and to neighboring countries have sleeping cars as well as coaches. Some of the express trains have lounge cars, where passengers may watch television. Passengers

Railroads have been an important means of transportation in Germany since the middle of the nineteenth century. Today, West Germany has one of the world's most efficient railroad systems.

may travel first, second, or third class, depending on how much they wish to pay.

Roads in West Germany. West Germany's highways are among the finest in Europe. Modern superhighways called autobahns spread like broad ribbons across the land. It is possible to travel along these highways for miles without stopping or even slowing down.

More and more West Germans are buying automobiles, but many still travel by bus, bicycle, or motorcycle. In the cities, most workers travel by bicycle or on crowded streetcars to reach their work. Groups of bicyclists of all ages are a common sight on the roads of West Germany. Bicycles are not permitted on the autobahns, however.

Air travel in West Germany. The West Germans were not permitted to have their own airline for a number of years following World War II. In 1953, however, after the restrictions had been lifted, a government-owned company called Lufthansa was formed in West Germany. The East German government has also formed its own airline, called Interflug. The map on the opposite page shows the routes used by these

At a West German airport. The West Germans were not permitted to have their own airline after World War II. In 1953, after the restrictions were lifted, a government-owned airline called Lufthansa was formed. East Germany has since formed its own airline, also.

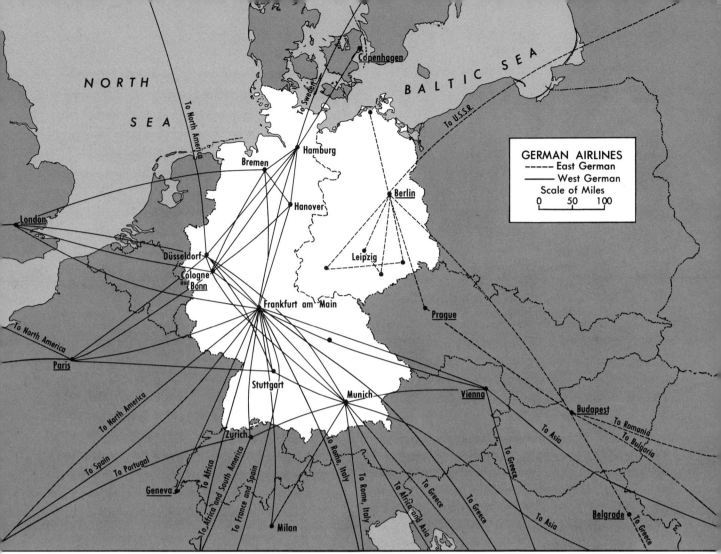

German airlines. West Germany has a more dense network of internal air routes than East Germany. The two parts of divided Germany are not connected by German airlines.

two airlines. West Germany is served by the airlines of other countries as well as by its own Lufthansa.

Communication in West Germany. In addition to its modern system of transportation, West Germany has a good communication system. News is spread by means of newspapers, magazines, and radio and television broadcasts. The government operates the postal service, as well as telegraph, telephone, radio, and television communications. Most West German families have radios, and many own television sets. Listeners enjoy musical and sports programs, dramas, and news broadcasts much as people do in

the United States. There are also special children's programs. Radio owners pay a small monthly fee to help finance broadcasting, since very little broadcast time is paid for by advertising.

Transportation and communication in East Germany. Like West Germany, East Germany has a good network of railroads, roads, and waterways. As you learned earlier, it also has its own airline. The traffic in the two parts of Germany differs in important ways, however. Only about seven out of every hundred barges and boats on East Germany's canals and rivers have motors.

RADIO FREE EUROPE

A link with freedom. Each day thousands of people in five eastern European countries listen to special radio programs from the free world. These programs are heard over Radio Free Europe, a private American radio network. Radio Free Europe broadcasts to the people in Poland, Czechoslovakia, Hungary, Romania, and Bulgaria. It is a link with freedom for these people, whose radio programs and newspapers are controlled by their Communist governments.

Radio Free Europe offers its listeners a wide variety of programs. The most important of these are accurate news broadcasts, since facts are often distorted or omitted in Communist newspapers and radio reports. Each news program on Radio Free Europe is followed by a news analysis that helps listeners understand how current events affect their particular countries. There are also special programs for housewives, children, students, and workers. Sports events, religious programs, and discussions on art and literature are also broadcast.

How Radio Free Europe operates. Radio Free Europe, which began to broadcast on July 4, 1950, actually consists of five stations, or broadcasting departments. The headquarters of these stations is located in Munich, West Germany. Each station broadcasts to one of the five countries in the language or languages spoken there. Many people on the Radio Free Europe staff are refugees, who work as reporters, writers, or announcers.

Communist reactions to Radio Free Europe. Although it is not illegal for the people in the five countries to listen to Radio Free Europe, the Communists do much to discourage listening. They condemn Radio Free Europe in newspapers, magazines, pamphlets, and in official speeches. They are also more apt to give job promotions or better apartments to people who do not listen to its programs.

The main attempt the Communists make to silence Radio Free Europe is by jamming its programs. This is done by special electrical equipment called jammers, which create buzzing and whistling sounds. Although this violates international radio laws, the Communists spend about 100 million dollars a year for jamming — about ten times the amount Radio Free Europe spends to broadcast its programs.

In spite of jamming, listeners are able to hear about 90 percent of Radio Free Europe's programs. This is because its engineers broadcast a program over five to seven transmitters at the same time, which makes it possible for the program to be heard on more than one station. The Communists are unable to jam all these stations at once.

Similar radio stations. There are other radio stations that are similar to Radio Free Europe. The largest of these is Voice of America, an official station of the United States government. It broadcasts all over the world, in 36 different languages. Another official station of the United States government is Radio in the American Sector, which broadcasts to the people in East Germany. A privately owned station, Radio Liberty, broadcasts to the Soviet Union in Russian and 16 other languages spoken by the people there.

Broadcasting from Munich

In comparison, about half of the inland water traffic in West Germany is motorized.

East Germany's roads seem deserted compared to West Germany's. Although there are some trucks, buses, and horse-drawn carts, there are comparatively few automobiles. People who wish to travel in East Germany usually go by bus or bicycle.

All public transportation and communication facilities in East Germany are controlled by the government. Private ownership of these services is not permitted. Newspapers may only print government-approved news, and people are discouraged from listening to radio broadcasts from non-Communist countries. (See opposite page.)

Trade and travel between East and West Germany. Before Germany was divided, roads, railroads, and waterways connected all parts of the country. Today, there is heavy traffic between West Berlin and West Germany, but very little between East and West Germany. The Communists have blocked most of the transportation routes at the border between these two areas. A few roads, railroads, and waterways remain open. These transportation routes are used mainly by barges, trucks, and freight trains.

Travel restrictions made by the East German government discourage many people from traveling between the two parts of divided Germany. East Germans who wish to go to West Germany

East German workers on their way home. There are few cars in East Germany, so people who wish to travel usually go by bus or bicycle. Bicycles are also a common sight in West Germany.

Crossing a border checkpoint. Most of the transportation routes connecting East and West Germany are blocked at the border.

must get special permission from their government, and this is very difficult to obtain. Although the West German government does not have any restrictions of this kind, West Germans who wish to go to East Germany must get permission from the East German government. They may not travel about freely in East Germany while they are there, and when they return home they must cross the border at the same place they entered.

East and West Germany still carry on some trade. West Germany sells iron, steel, and machinery to East Germany. In exchange, it buys lignite, crude oil, textiles, and chemicals. Arrangements for this trade are made between special committees appointed by each government.

Checking Your Understanding

Give as many facts as possible to prove each of the following statements:
1. West Germany has an excellent system of transportation.
2. Traffic on East Germany's rivers, canals, and highways differs from that in West Germany.
3. Trade and travel between East and West Germany are limited.

Drawing Conclusions

The following questions are not specifically answered in the chapter. As a class, study each question carefully and draw conclusions as to what the answer might reasonably be. You may want to use outside sources in carrying out this project. Refer to the suggestions on pages 178 and 179 to help you locate information. The suggestions on page 184 will help make your discussion successful.
1. Why is it necessary for any country to have a good system of transportation if it wishes to develop industrially?
2. What geographical features of Germany have been favorable for the development of a good system of transportation?
3. Why do East German roads seem deserted compared to those in West Germany?
4. Why is bicycle travel more common in East and West Germany than in the United States?

For Further Understanding

Each day we are influenced by some form of propaganda. To learn more about propaganda, answer the questions below. You will want to refer to the suggestions on pages 179 and 180.
1. What is propaganda?
2. Why is propaganda usually successful?
3. What are some of the ways propaganda can be spread?
4. Make a list of the ways you are influenced by propaganda in one day.

Part 4

People and Culture

A carved altar in a German church. The Germans have a long cultural heritage and are noted for their artistic and scientific achievements.

A street in Frankfurt am Main, West Germany. The people in West Germany enjoy more freedom and a higher standard of living than the people in East Germany.

In the heart of Frankfurt am Main, West Germany. Germany is one of the most densely populated parts of Europe. About 80 percent of Germany's people live in West Germany.

14 People

A Study Guide

Thoughts To Help You

Like people throughout the world, the people of Germany have been strongly influenced by the events of the past. As you study this chapter see what effect history has had on each of the following in Germany:
1. language
2. religion
3. living standards
4. the migrations of people

If one third of the people in the United States lived in the state of Montana, it would be almost as crowded as Germany is today. Germany has a population of more than 74 million. Over 57 million of these people live in West Germany. The rest live in East Germany.

What the people of Germany look like. The descendants of many different groups of people live in Germany. Through the years, these groups have intermarried. As a result, there are short, medium, and tall people in Germany. There are also people with blond hair and people with dark hair. Many tall, blond people live in northern Germany, and many short, dark-haired people live in southern Germany. There are numerous exceptions in both areas, however.

Language. The German language is not spoken in the same way in all parts of Germany. For example, the word *"Ich,"* meaning "I," is pronounced "ish" in the north, while in the south, it is pronounced "ikh." These regional differences in speech are called dialects. There are two main groups of dialects in Germany. One of these groups is spoken in

In northern Germany, many of the people are tall and blond. In the southern highlands, many of the people are short and have brown hair and dark eyes.

northern Germany and the other is spoken in the southern highlands.

In school, the Germans learn to speak and read a standard form of German. This standard form is also used in newspapers, books, and movies, and by radio and television stations. The type of German that Martin Luther used in his translation of the Bible influenced the development of the standard form of German.

City people and villagers. The majority of the German people live either in cities or medium-sized towns. Their way of life is much the same as that of people in other parts of the Western world. Only about one fourth of the people in Germany live on farms or in farming villages. In some isolated country areas, the people still live in much the same

Shoppers in a West German town. Most Germans live either in cities or medium-sized towns.

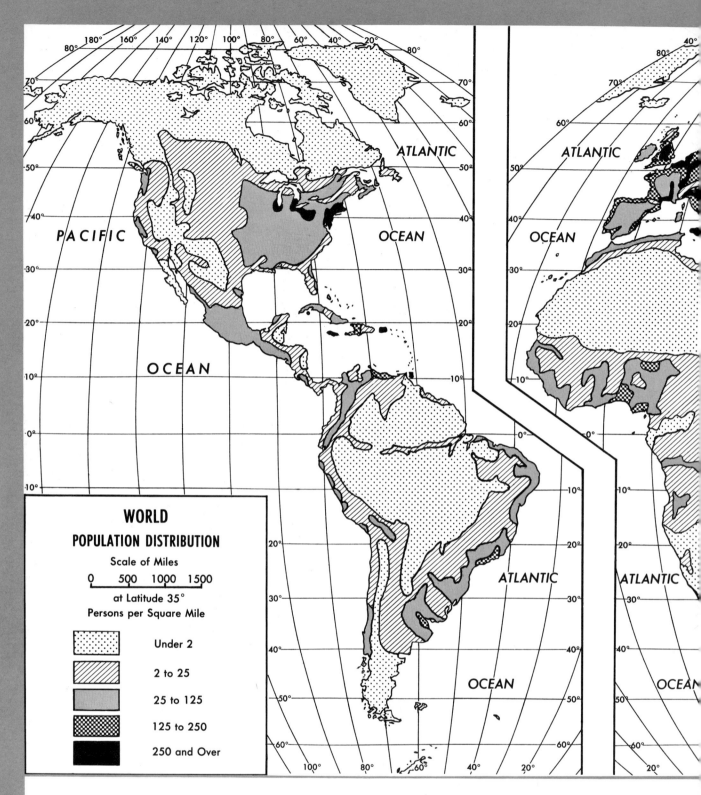

WORLD
POPULATION DISTRIBUTION

Scale of Miles

0   500   1000   1500

at Latitude 35°

Persons per Square Mile

░░░	Under 2
⫽⫽⫽	2 to 25
▒▒▒	25 to 125
▦▦▦	125 to 250
███	250 and Over

More than three billion people live in the world today. If all these people were evenly distributed over the earth, there would be about fifty people to each square mile of land. The map above shows that this is not the case, however. Some areas are very crowded, and others are almost empty. The three most heavily populated parts of the world are East Asia, South Asia, and Europe. All three are located on the landmass of Eurasia, one of the world's oldest homes of civilization. All three of these also have land and climate that is suitable for farming.

The world's population has more than quadrupled since 1800. Medical advances, improvements in sanitation, and increased food supplies help to explain this increase. Death rates have fallen in most areas, while birthrates have remained high.

The population of the world is still expanding. Over the period from 1950 to 1963, the rate of increase was about 2.2 percent annually. If this rate

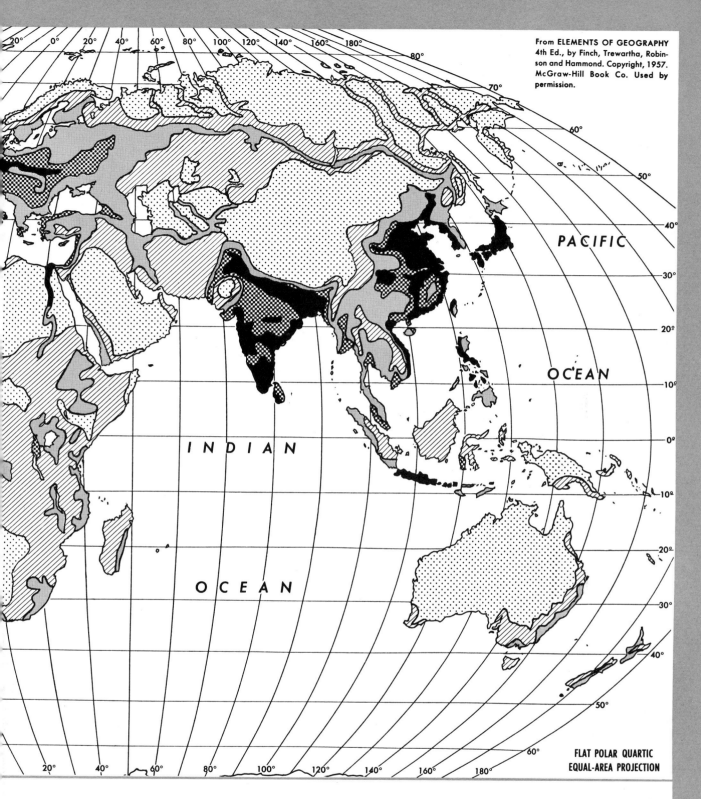

From ELEMENTS OF GEOGRAPHY
4th Ed., by Finch, Trewartha, Robinson and Hammond. Copyright, 1957.
McGraw-Hill Book Co. Used by permission.

PACIFIC

OCEAN

INDIAN

OCEAN

FLAT POLAR QUARTIC
EQUAL-AREA PROJECTION

of growth continues it is estimated that the world's population will double every thirty-five years.

In general, the population of the underdeveloped parts of the world is increasing more rapidly than the population of the industrialized parts. For example, it is estimated that the number of people in Europe, outside the Soviet Union, increased at a yearly rate of .9 percent from 1950 to 1963. During these years in Africa, however, the annual rate of population increase was 3.3 percent. This difference is due mainly to the fact that birthrates are higher in underdeveloped areas.

The rapidly expanding population of the world presents one of the greatest challenges facing mankind. Although the world's food supply can be greatly increased, it probably is not unlimited. Some way must be found to bring the world's birthrates in balance with its present low death rates if mankind is to achieve its dream of a world free from want.

133

Traditional costumes. In most parts of Germany, traditional costumes are worn only on special occasions.

way their ancestors did. However, the differences between city people and country people are growing smaller. In most parts of Germany, the colorful costumes of former times are worn only on festive occasions.

Religion. In West Germany, less than half the people are Roman Catholics, and slightly more than half are Protestants. Many of the Protestants are refugees from East Germany, where Protestantism is the main form of Christianity. The largest Protestant organization in Germany is the Evangelical Church of Germany, formed after World War II by several Protestant denominations. Although the great majority of Germans

An Evangelical Church service in West Germany. In West Germany slightly more than half the people are Protestant and most of the rest are Roman Catholic. In East Germany there are many more Protestants than Catholics.

are either Protestant or Roman Catholic, some hold other religious beliefs. Important among these people are the Jews. When Hitler came to power, there were about one-half million Jews in Germany. Today, however, there are only about fifty thousand. The murder of hundreds of thousands of German Jews in Nazi concentration camps was responsible for this decline.

Christians in Germany have also suffered persecutions. In Hitler's time, church leaders who criticized the actions of the Nazi government received harsh treatment. Today, pressure is being placed on the people of East Germany to accept the Communist teaching that there is no God. Young people who belong to church groups are sometimes prevented from enrolling in schools, and religious leaders are often arrested. The Communist government also tries to prevent any contact between Christians in East and West Germany.

Standard of living. In addition to enjoying less religious freedom, East Germans have a lower standard of living than West Germans. Little new housing is available in East Germany. In addition, many goods that people would like to buy are scarce. Some goods that are for sale to East Germans, such as shoes and clothing, are often poorly made.

West Germany, on the other hand, has one of the highest standards of living in Europe. Stores are well supplied with goods people want to buy, and the average worker earns enough to buy attractive clothing, good food, and some luxury items, such as a television set. About seventy out of every thousand West Germans own cars as compared

A street market in East Germany. The East Germans do not have as high a standard of living as the people of West Germany.

Exploring Population

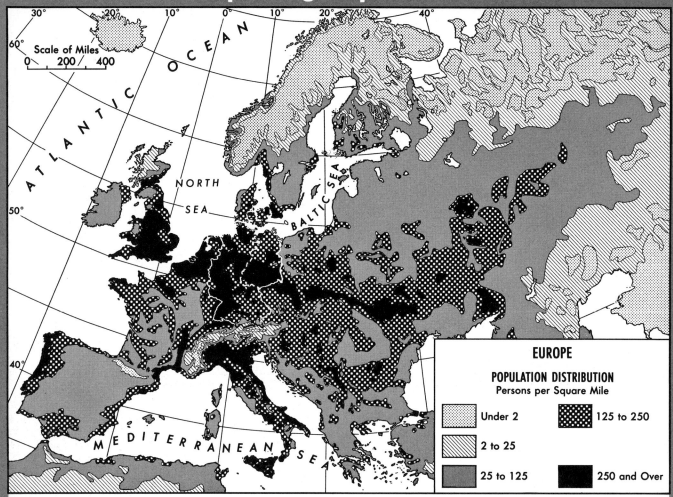

EUROPE

POPULATION DISTRIBUTION
Persons per Square Mile

Under 2	125 to 250
2 to 25	
25 to 125	250 and Over

Europe is the world's most densely populated continent. Europe is the home of about 600 million people, more than live in the continents of North and South America combined. Europe's population has reached this vast size in a comparatively brief period. At the time of the Roman Empire, scholars estimate that only about 34 million people lived in Europe. By A.D. 500, after the fall of Rome, this number had fallen possibly as low as 20 million. During the Middle Ages, Europe's population began to increase. Although this increase was irregular, and interrupted by disasters such as the plagues, Europe's population had reached approximately 100 million by 1650. In the next three centuries, however, this figure increased sixfold. This rise in population may be traced to the effects of the Industrial Revolution — larger, more dependable, and more varied food supplies, increase in trade, and advances in medicine and sanitation.

Today, Europe's population is not growing as rapidly as that of other continents. Between 1950 and 1963, the estimated annual increase in population in Europe, outside the Soviet Union, was .9 percent, lower than any other continent.

Divided Germany is one of the most heavily populated parts of Europe. East and West Germany together have a larger population than any country in Europe except the European portion of the Soviet Union. Although Germany is only about the size of Montana, it has more than 74 million people. This is more than one third as many as live in the United States. About 80 percent of these people live in West Germany.

In a West German home. Although the standard of living in East and West Germany is different, the people are still alike in many ways. As a whole, the Germans are home-loving, industrious people who have made good use of what nature has given them.

with less than ten out of every thousand East Germans.

Many Germans are refugees. More than three million East Germans have become so dissatisfied with life in East Germany that they have fled to West Germany. In addition, more than ten million Germans who were forced by the Communists to leave their homes in other parts of eastern Europe after World War II have come to West Germany. Altogether, about one out of every five West Germans is a refugee. Many of these refugees entered West Germany with few, if any, possessions. The West German government has helped these people obtain jobs and homes.

A considerably smaller number of people have chosen to leave West Germany to live in East Germany. Some of these people are members of the Communist Party. Others are East Germans who returned home because of families they had left behind, or because life in West Germany was not as good as they expected.

What the German people are like. Although the standard of living in East Germany differs from that in West Germany, the people in both areas are still alike in many ways. It is risky to say that any one group of people has character traits that are the same. However, it is fair to say that the Germans as a whole are a home-loving and an industrious people. They have shown their hard-working ways by the speed with which they reconstructed cities bombed in World War II. They are also thrifty, and make the most of what nature has given them. One needs only to look at the beautiful parks and to see the families on their Sunday afternoon hikes to know that Germans are lovers of nature.

Checking Your Understanding
In addition to the text, use the maps in this chapter to answer the following questions:
1. Where do the majority of the German people live?
2. Why has the world's population increased so greatly since 1800?
3. How does the combined population of East and West Germany compare in size to the population of the United States?

Learning More About the German Language
About 100 million people speak German as their native language. Using this book and other sources, write a report about the German language. You may want to organize your report in the following way:
1. a section telling where the German language is spoken and why it is an important language
2. a section describing some of the characteristics of the language, such as capitalization and word order
3. a section comparing High German and Low German

Use the suggestions on pages 178-182 to help you locate and evaluate information and to write a well-written report.

Understanding Human Problems
Sometimes the problems people face cannot be solved easily. Human emotions and feelings are often involved in making decisions. Imagine you are a member of a family in East Germany that has an opportunity to flee to the West. What would your decision be? Now, as a class, rethink the problem.

Several students can imagine they are members of the East German family described below. These students can discuss the situation as if they are the actual family members, and come to a decision as a family.

Father. The father is a doctor. At one time he was a very important civic leader in the city where they live. He has spent his life serving the city and the people here. Yet, he does not believe in the Communist form of government.

Mother. The mother wants what is best for each member of the family.

Older Son. The older son is a university graduate and works for the government. He has a promising career ahead of him.

Younger Son. The younger son attends a university. He has an inquiring mind and longs for more freedom in his studies.

Older Daughter. The older daughter is not sure life would be better in West Germany.

Younger Daughter. The younger daughter hears a lot about life in West Germany. She and her friends envy the style of clothes and the fun that West Germans of their age seem to have.

Grandmother. The grandmother is ill. She has raised her family here. Her husband died and was buried here.

After the family problem has been investigated and a decision reached, discuss the following questions with your classmates:
1. What decision did the family finally make? Why?
2. Have your first ideas changed? Why?

Towers and walls in the city of Nuremberg were built during the Middle Ages, when cities were generally fortified for protection. Most of the cities in Germany were founded centuries ago.

15 Cities

A Study Guide

Thoughts To Help You

A visitor to Germany's cities can find much to remind him of this divided country's past. In your study of Germany's cities, look for the following:

1. evidence that there was disorder in the German countryside during the Middle Ages
2. evidence that Germany suffered terrible destruction during World War II
3. evidence that Germany is a divided country

Most cities in Germany are very old. Most German cities were founded centuries ago. Some began as small communities that grew up outside the walls of fortresses during the early part of the Middle Ages.* Others began as market settlements established by princely families to encourage trade. German towns in the Middle Ages were usually surrounded by walls to protect the people from attacks by their warlike neighbors. Because land was scarce inside the walls

*See glossary

139

Main Cities Of Germany

NORTH SEA

BALTIC SEA

D E N M A R K

Kiel

Rostock

Lübeck

Wilhelmshaven • Bremerhaven

Hamburg

Oldenburg

Bremen

Elbe R.

POLAND

NETHERLANDS

Osnabrück

Münster

Bielefeld

Weser R.

Hanover

Brunswick

Salzgitter

Magdeburg

Potsdam

Berlin

Oder R.

Oder R.

Neisse R.

Duisburg

Dortmund

Essen

Düsseldorf

Ruhr R.

Kassel

Halle

Leipzig

Dresden

Cologne

Aachen

Bonn

Rhine R.

Erfurt

Karl-Marx-Stadt (Chemnitz)

Zwickau

Elbe R.

BELGIUM

LUX.

Wiesbaden

Frankfurt am Main

Offenbach

Mainz

Darmstadt

Würzburg

Main R.

CZECHOSLOVAKIA

Mannheim

Ludwigshafen am Rhein

Heidelberg

Saarbrücken

Karlsruhe

Nuremberg

Stuttgart

Regensburg

Danube R.

FRANCE

Rhine R.

Augsburg

Danube R.

Freiburg

Munich

SWITZERLAND

AUSTRIA

ITALY

RUHR AREA

Scale of Miles

0   10   20   30

Recklinghausen

Wanne-Eickel   Herne

Bottrop   Gelsenkirchen

Oberhausen   Essen   Bochum   Dortmund

Duisburg   Mülheim an der Ruhr   Ruhr R.

Hagen

Krefeld

Rhine R.

Düsseldorf   Wuppertal

München-Gladbach   Remscheid   Solingen

140

MAIN CITIES

Scale of Miles

0   25   50   75

• 100,000 to 250,000

● 250,000 to 500,000

◎ 500,000 to 1,000,000

◉ 1,000,000 and Over

of the towns, the houses were built very close together. The streets in these old towns were narrow and winding. Often, a majestic cathedral overlooked the open market square in the center of a town.

Sections of old towns still stand in the heart of some German cities. Their tall, narrow houses and crooked streets remind us of the Middle Ages. A tourist who visits one of these old sections today may feel as though he had returned to the days of medieval* merchants and craftsmen. The beautiful cathedral still overlooks the busy market square. On market days, vendors display their goods much as the merchants, craftsmen, and peddlers did in the Middle Ages.

Some of Germany's cities, like Heidelberg, have changed little since medieval days, but many others have become large and modern. In some, a boulevard marks the course that the old town wall once followed. Beyond the boulevard may be the new business district, with modern stores and office buildings. Here also may be found theaters, concert halls, museums, and art galleries.

In another part of the city rise the tall smokestacks of factories and mills. In some cities, homes for the workers have been built near the factories.

In still another part of the city is the main residential area. Here are rows and rows of apartment buildings. Many city people in Germany live in apartment buildings or in smaller two- or three-family dwellings.

Outside most cities in Germany are many well-tended gardens. These gardens belong to families who live in the cities. Often the people go out to work in their gardens on Sunday afternoon.

141

Many cities damaged in the war have been rebuilt. During World War II, the cities of Germany were severely damaged by Allied bombing raids. Whole sections of such large industrial centers as Berlin, Essen, Cologne, Hanover, Kassel, and Frankfurt am Main were destroyed. The war wrecked historic buildings, as well as churches, homes, and apartment buildings. Many factories and mills were also left in ruins.

In West Germany, the work of reconstruction began almost as soon as the war was over. The German people worked with amazing speed and energy. Tons of wreckage were cleared away. Where rubble once littered the cities, there are now modern apartment buildings, stores, offices, and huge new factories.

World War II ruins in Hamburg. The cities of Germany were severely damaged in World War II.

The port city of Hamburg in West Germany is located on the Elbe River. Hamburg, Munich, and Berlin are the three largest cities in Germany. Each has a population of more than a million.

In East Germany's cities, much of the war damage has also been repaired. However, a considerable number of ruined buildings can still be seen in these cities.

Important cities of East and West Germany. The largest and most important city in Germany is Berlin. (See map on page 140.) More than three million people live here. Although located in East Germany, Berlin is politically divided between East and West Germany. The eastern part of the city has a Communist government, and the western part has a democratic government, protected by the United States, Great Britain,

and France. Chapter 6 contains additional information about Berlin.

Germany has two other cities with populations of more than one million people each. One is the port city of Hamburg, in the north, which is described on pages 120 and 121. The other is Munich, in the south. Both of these cities are located in West Germany.

Munich's German name, *München*, means "place of the monks." This beautiful city grew up near a community founded by monks from the nearby cloister of Tegernsee. It became the capital of Bavaria in the Middle Ages, and grew into an important cultural

The beautiful city of Munich, in the southern part of West Germany, is an important cultural and industrial city. It is noted for its production of church bells and stained glass.

city. Munich is also a commercial and industrial city. It is noted for its production of church bells and stained glass for church windows. Its breweries are also famous.

Next to Berlin, the largest city located in East Germany is Leipzig. (See map on page 140.) Leipzig is an important manufacturing city. Among the goods manufactured here are textiles, plastics, electrical appliances, and steel products. Leipzig also is well known as a city of art and learning. It has fine museums, art galleries, and educational institutions. Many great musicians lived here, among them Bach, Mendelssohn, and Schumann. Before World War II, Leipzig was noted for its many publishing houses. Today, only a few of these are still in operation.

Leipzig was also famous as a trading city before World War II. Partly because of its location at the crossroads of important trade routes, great trade

Visitors to a Leipzig trade fair. The second largest city in East Germany is Leipzig. Before World War II, businessmen from many countries came to the great trade fairs held here. Today, these fairs are mainly used for displaying industrial goods made in Communist countries.

fairs were held here. These were attended by businessmen from many countries. Since the war, trade between eastern and western Europe has decreased, and the Leipzig trade fairs have mainly been used to display industrial products made in Communist countries.

Another of East Germany's important cities is Dresden. Before the war, during which it suffered great damage, Dresden was considered one of the most beautiful cities in the world. Since the war, wide streets and modern buildings have been constructed in Dresden. However, the old part of the city has been rebuilt to look much as it did hundreds of years ago. Like Leipzig, Dresden is well known for its fine museums, art galleries, and educational institutions. It is also an important manufacturing city.

Dresden is an important cultural and industrial city of East Germany. It suffered severe damage in the war, but has been extensively rebuilt.

Checking Your Understanding
Using the map, captions, and text in this chapter, answer the following:
1. Name and locate three German cities with populations of more than one million each.
2. Name and locate three German cities with populations of 250,000 to 500,000 each.
3. What features of medieval towns can still be found in some German cities?
4. Describe what you might see in a large, modern German city.
5. What effect did World War II have on many German cities?

History and German Cities
Many German cities are associated with a particular historical event. Write a paragraph about each of the following:
1. Munich as the scene of the Nazi Party's rise to power
2. Nuremberg as the scene of war crime trials after World War II

3. Augsburg as a medieval center of trade and as a scene of the Augsburg Confession
4. Potsdam as the scene of the Potsdam Conference following World War II

The suggestions on pages 178-182 will help you locate and evaluate information and prepare an interesting report.

Learning About German Cathedrals
Many German cities have beautiful cathedrals that were built during the Middle Ages. These cathedrals were designed mainly in the Romanesque and Gothic styles of architecture. Write a report describing these styles of architecture. The suggestions on pages 178 and 179 will help you locate information you need. You can also refer to the suggestions on pages 181 and 182 to help you write a good report. If possible, illustrate your report with pictures or sketches of Romanesque and Gothic cathedrals in Germany.

Students in a basic school in West Germany. The purpose of education in West Germany is to prepare students to participate in a modern, democratic society.

16 Education

A Study Guide

A Problem To Solve

The goal of Communists everywhere is to bring the world under communism. Education in Communist countries is aimed toward the achievement of this goal. <u>How does education in East Germany further the goal of communism?</u> In forming hypotheses, you will want to consider the following:

1. how the East German schools try to shape students' attitudes
2. how the East German students are prepared to be effective workers

See TO THE STUDENT, pages 6-7.

The purpose of education is to prepare students for life in their society. In democracies, where people take part in the government and decide for themselves how they want to work and live, the goal of education is to prepare students to think for themselves. However, in dictatorships, where the government controls people's lives, education also is controlled by the central government, and students are taught to follow government orders without question.

Education in East Germany

East Germany's leaders are determined to create a truly Communist nation. One way they are trying to do this is by controlling all forms of education. No private schools of any kind are permitted in East Germany. All textbooks are published by one government-owned publishing house, and contain only what the government wants students to know. The Ministry of Public Education, a department of the central government, decides what courses each school will give and how they are to be taught. Teachers must follow instructions from the central government.

Goals of education in East Germany. The main goal of education in East Germany is to develop students into loyal Communist citizens. As the East German Minister of Education in 1956 said, "Education for patriotism, for unlimited devotion and unshakeable fidelity to our Republic, to the cause of socialism, to the working classes and their party must be the central task of all education."

Another major goal of schools in East Germany is to prepare students to be good Communist workers. East German schools try to give young people a survey of the entire economic system and to provide them with information about each branch of the economy. Communist educators call this "polytechnic" training. A great deal of the East German student's polytechnic training is done outside the classroom. Programs such as the "day in industry," in which the student spends one day a week during the school year in a factory or some other productive plant, provide practical experience.

How East Germany's school system is organized. In East Germany, all students are provided with the same type of education through the tenth grade. After tenth grade, the student has his choice of different types of training, several of which prepare him to go on to a university. The following paragraphs discuss the different levels of education in East Germany.

Kindergarten. Children may begin their education in East Germany when they are three years old. In kindergartens run by the government or by factories, children begin to learn how the goods that people need are produced. They look at pictures of farmers and factory workers and learn to use simple tools. They are also taught to believe that what their government does is right.

Elementary school. When they are six years old, East German children enter ten-year elementary schools. In the lower four grades, they study reading, writing, arithmetic, drawing, music, and physical education. In addition to these subjects, students in the upper grades study history, geography, science, and Russian.

Throughout elementary school, students are taught the political beliefs that the government wants them to hold. In a class called community study, fourth graders take trips through their community, learning about its history and geography. These trips are designed to strengthen the student's belief that the government is doing a good job of running the country. As a part of their

East German students. In East Germany, all students are provided with the same type of education through the tenth grade.

polytechnic training, students in the lower grades care for crops in the school garden. Upper-grade students take part in the "day in industry."

Post-elementary education. Students who graduate from tenth grade must continue some form of education until they are eighteen years old. Those who wish to take jobs in farming or industry attend vocational schools. Vocational training also is required of students who plan to go on to a university.

There are several ways that students may obtain the courses leading to the certificate necessary for entering a university. These students may attend regular or evening high schools. They may also go to vocational schools that offer university-preparatory courses.

Higher education. East Germany has six universities, and a large number of technical schools that grant diplomas in specialized studies, such as mining and teaching. To be admitted to an institution of higher learning, students must show wholehearted agreement with government beliefs. Political education courses are required in East German universities, and students spend nearly one third of their time studying Marxism-Leninism* and other politically oriented subjects.

The East German government claims the right and duty to control higher education. The State Secretariat of Higher Education, a department of the central government, decides which courses students should take. It also controls the appointment of all professors. A number of outstanding German professors, dissatisfied with government interference in higher education, have fled to West Germany.

*See glossary

In an East German high school. Schools in East Germany give students a survey of their economic system and provide them with information about each branch of the economy. Communist educators call this "polytechnic" training.

Other schools. East Germany has other schools in addition to those already mentioned. There are special schools for handicapped children. Children who are outstanding athletes may attend sport schools, which emphasize physical training in addition to other subjects.

Activities outside of school. The East German government controls as much of the students' after-school time as possible. "Homes" are provided by the government where students whose parents work may spend their after-school hours doing homework and working on hobbies. There are also government-sponsored clubs that provide students with the opportunity to take hikes, have dances, and take part in other activities. The main purpose of these organizations, however, is to educate young people in the government's political beliefs.

Although membership in government-sponsored youth organizations is voluntary, it is difficult for young people to avoid joining. Those who are not members cannot take part in the activities their schoolmates enjoy. Also, people who have not been members may have difficulty getting jobs when they are adults.

After World War II, the United States and other democratic countries helped West Germany establish schools that would prepare West German young people for citizenship in a democracy. Today, West German students are encouraged to ask questions, to search for reasons, and to express their views freely. Educators in West Germany try to arouse a feeling of political responsibility in their students, but do not tell them what political beliefs to hold.

Education in West Germany is not under the control of the central government. Instead, each state has the responsibility of maintaining public schools in

A Catholic kindergarten. After kindergarten, West German students enter basic elementary school.

its area. Private schools under state supervision are also permitted in West Germany.

Kindergarten. West German children from the ages of three to six may attend kindergartens run by churches, welfare societies, communes,* or private individuals. These kindergartens prepare the children for first grade and help them to feel that they belong to a community.

Basic elementary school. West German children enter basic elementary school when they are six years old. This basic schooling lasts four years in some areas and six years in others. During their basic schooling, children study reading, writing, and arithmetic, and learn how to use their time creatively. In addition, they learn about their community. If their parents wish, children may also attend classes in religion.

After basic elementary schooling is completed, West German children take a series of important examinations that help decide what type of education they will receive next. Depending on the results of these examinations and on the wishes of their parents, students go on to later elementary school, to middle school, or to *gymnasium.* (See page 152.) Since the occupations that students will hold as adults are largely determined by the type of education they receive, these examinations have a far-reaching effect.

Later elementary school. More than seven tenths of the students who take the examinations after basic elementary school continue elementary schooling through the eighth or ninth grade. These

Students in a technical school. After completing basic school, West German students take examinations that help determine their future course of study. Most continue elementary school through the eighth or ninth grade, then go on for vocational training.

students will later attend vocational-training schools. During the last years of elementary school, pupils study the German language, religion, arithmetic, folklore, and geography. They also have classes in history, science, drawing, singing, and physical education. Students who want to may take a foreign language.

Middle school. About one tenth of the students who take the examinations after basic elementary school go directly to six-year middle schools. These middle school students will later attend vocational-training schools that prepare them for positions that are higher than those elementary school graduates can expect

to hold. Among the most important subjects middle school students take are the social sciences, mathematics, and science. Study of a foreign language is also required.

Vocational education. Most students who complete elementary school or middle school go on for special vocational training. Some take part-time jobs, where they receive training while they work. In addition, several days each week they have classes in language, social science, religion, and subjects that will help them in their chosen vocations. Other students enter full-time professional schools where they learn the skills needed to do office work, housekeeping, or other jobs. All young people must continue some form of schooling until they are eighteen years old, or have passed certain examinations.

Gymnasium. About seventeen out of every hundred students taking the examinations after basic elementary school go on to *gymnasium,* which prepares them for university studies. There are three types of *gymnasiums*. The first type of school stresses the classical languages, Latin and Greek. The second stresses the modern languages, English and French, in addition to Latin. The third places special emphasis on mathematics and science. Some students who are not able to attend *gymnasium* on a regular basis attend night classes to qualify for entrance into a university.

Higher education. West Germany has eighteen universities. It also has several institutions where students may receive the education needed for jobs in such fields as mining and veterinary medicine. In addition, there are a number of religious colleges. Both the professors and the students in West German institutions of higher learning enjoy freedom in their search for knowledge.

Other schools. West Germany has other schools in addition to those already discussed. Handicapped children may attend special schools. There are "people's universities" where adults may take evening classes. Also, trade unions, churches, and other private organizations in West Germany provide opportunities for education.

Ludwig Maximilian University in Munich. West Germany has eighteen universities. To qualify for entrance to these universities, West German students attend high schools called "gymnasiums."

Checking Your Understanding

1. What is the purpose of education?
2. In what ways does the East German government control education?
3. What are the goals of education in East Germany?
4. What social activities does the government of East Germany provide for its young people?
5. What disadvantages face East German young people who do not join clubs organized by the government?
6. How do West German educators try to prepare students for life in a democracy?
7. What are the three types of *gymnasiums* in West Germany?

Increasing Your Understanding

The educational systems in East and West Germany differ from each other in several ways. Use the information in this book and in other sources to write a report that traces the schooling of a bright student in East Germany from elementary school through university study. Include what courses he would take and what schools he would attend. Then, trace the schooling of a bright student in West Germany in the same way. When you have finished, point out the ways that the two systems differ from each other. The suggestions on pages 178-180 will help you to find and evaluate information. Refer to the suggestions on pages 181 and 182 to help you write a good report.

A Discussion On Educational Aims

In the United States, the purposes of education are generally these:

1. to acquire basic knowledge and skills
2. to learn to think reasonably and logically
3. to learn to be a responsible citizen
4. to develop as an individual
5. to prepare for an occupation
6. to develop moral character

In a class discussion, compare and contrast the educational system in a Communist society such as East Germany with the educational system in the United States. Are the goals of these societies similar? How does each society try to reach its goals?

The suggestions on page 184 will help to make your discussion successful.

Learning More About Education in Europe

The educational systems in Europe and in the United States have been greatly influenced by great writers, thinkers, and educators. Choose three of the men listed below and read about them. Write a report telling what influence each man had on education in Europe. The suggestions on pages 178-182 will help you to find and evaluate information and organize your material into a good report.

Francis Bacon
John Amos Comenius
Denis Diderot
Desiderius Erasmus
John Locke
John Milton
Johann Heinrich Pestalozzi
Jean Jacques Rousseau

Learning by Working Together

As a class, you can study the history of education in Europe. Your class may want to divide into committees. Each committee can study one of the following:

1. education in Ancient Greece
2. education in Ancient Rome
3. education in the Middle Ages
4. education during the Renaissance and the Reformation (1400's and 1500's)
5. education during the Age of Reason (1600's and 1700's)
6. education in the 1800's

You may want to think about the following questions:

a. What was education like during the particular period?
b. What famous men influenced education at that time?
c. What important advances were made in education during that period?

The suggestions on pages 178 and 179 will help you to locate information. Each committee may want to share its information with the rest of the class. The suggestions on page 183 will help your committee work together successfully.

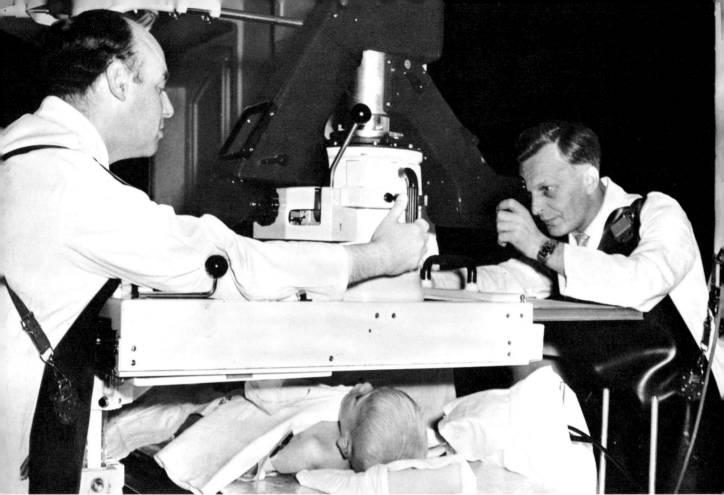

Using X-ray equipment to observe a heart disorder. X rays were discovered by a German professor of physics named Wilhelm Roentgen. German scientists have made valuable contributions to the world.

17 Scientists

A Study Guide

Thoughts To Help You
The Germans are among the world's most scientifically advanced people. As you read this chapter, look for the following information:

1. What contributions have German scientists made to the world?
2. What part did German scientists play in helping Germany become a leading industrial power?

One of medicine's most important discoveries was made accidentally late one November evening in 1895 by a professor of physics in a German university. Working in a darkened room, Professor Wilhelm Roentgen was experimenting with a vacuum tube, similar in principle to a television tube. He was using the tube to study the conduction of electricity through gases. To prevent the tube from emitting any light when it was charged with electricity, he had enclosed it in a black cardboard box. Suddenly, Roentgen was distracted by a glimmer of light on a nearby bench. A chemically treated paper screen lying on the bench was glowing. This glow appeared only when the tube was being supplied with the electric current.

As no light could escape from the box, Roentgen realized the glow was caused by unknown rays that were capable of passing through solid material. He experimented further and found that the bones in his hands made shadows on the paper when the rays passed through his hand. Because these rays were unknown to Roentgen, he named them X, which is the symbol scientists give to things unknown.

The X ray is now in widespread use for many different purposes. It enables physicians to examine all areas of the body by a painless and efficient technique. X-ray pictures are used to discover whether bones are broken and whether teeth or body organs are dis-

Wilhelm Roentgen received a Nobel prize for his discovery of X rays. As of 1963, fifty-six of these prizes had been awarded to Germans.

Robert Koch discovered the rodlike germ that causes tuberculosis. His discovery led to the control of the spread of this disease.

eased. X rays are also used in treating certain diseases, such as cancer. In addition, engineers use X rays to look for defects in steel and other metals. The discovery of the X ray gave mankind one of its most important tools in both medical diagnosis and physical research.

Another German whose discovery has benefited man was Robert Koch. For years people had lived in fear of the "white plague," as it was commonly called, for it meant almost certain death. No one knew the cause of this dread disease, now known as tuberculosis. In 1882, Robert Koch, using a microscope to study a sample of blood from a tubercular person, found the small rodlike germ that causes tuberculosis. His discovery led to the control of the spread of this disease.

Both Roentgen and Koch won Nobel prizes for their discoveries. Nobel prizes have been awarded since 1901 to men and women of many nations for their outstanding contributions to physics, chemistry, physiology and medicine, literature, and peace. It is interesting to note that as of 1963, fifty-six winners of the Nobel prize have been from Germany.

Many other German scientists have made great achievements, but have not received the Nobel prize. Four years before these awards were first granted, Rudolf Diesel, a German inventor, completed the engine that was later named after him. This engine was more efficient and more economical to run than other types of engines in use at the time. Also, it was a reliable engine and could operate for long periods of time with little attention. Today diesel engines are used to power trains, ships, and trucks, as well as being a source of industrial power.

The history of scientific achievement in Germany has not followed a steady course. In the early 1800's, Germany was not noted for its scientists. As the years passed, however, the universities of Germany developed into internationally famous centers of learning. Scientists from other countries were attracted to these universities, and their achievements further added to Germany's reputation as a scientific leader.

A diesel-powered train. Diesel engines, named for the German inventor Rudolf Diesel, are used to power trains, ships, and trucks. They are also used as a source of industrial power.

The Germans put their scientific knowledge to practical use, especially in the chemical industry. Before the start of World War I, Germany was practically unrivaled in every scientific field, and was almost the only producer of fine chemicals, dyes, and scientific instruments.

As the twentieth century progressed, Germany lost its position of scientific leadership. This was partly because of the hardships the Germans suffered during and after World War I, and partly because of the restrictions Hitler placed on freedom of thought. As a result, many German scientists left Germany and put their talents to use in other countries.

Some of Germany's outstanding scientists went to the United States. Among these was Albert Einstein, whose theory of relativity helped scientists gain a new understanding of the universe. According to Einstein's theory, matter and energy are different forms of the same reality. This understanding has made possible the use of atomic energy, both for peaceful purposes and for war.

Wernher von Braun (left), a scientist from Germany, is considered to be the world's leading rocket engineer. He now lives and works in the United States.

Although the Germans can no longer claim their former position of world leadership in the sciences, the influence of their great scientific heritage is still strong. In West Germany today, scientists are once again working in freedom.

Checking Your Understanding
1. Why was the discovery of the X ray so important?
2. What are the Nobel prizes?
3. What are the advantages of a diesel engine?
4. What factors weakened Germany's position of scientific leadership in the twentieth century?

German Scientists in America
The names of three German scientists who came to the United States from Germany are listed below. Read about these scientists and write a paragraph about each man. Tell what circumstances led him to come to America and what important contributions he made.

Albert Einstein
Wernher von Braun
Charles Proteus Steinmetz

The suggestions on pages 178-182 will help you to locate and evaluate information and to write a good paragraph.

West Berlin's new opera house was opened in 1961. It is one of many cultural buildings in Germany. The Germans are noted for their deep respect for cultural achievement.

18 Artists

A Study Guide

Thoughts To Help You

Germany has contributed much to the arts of the Western world. As you study this chapter, notice the following:

1. the number of German artists and works of art that are known by people throughout the Western world

2. the century in which most of Germany's outstanding artists lived and worked

3. how the actions of Hitler and the Communists have affected German artists

The Germans are noted for their deep respect for cultural achievement. Through the years, the Germans have produced many artists worthy of this respect. These artists have made important contributions to the arts of the Western world.

Writers. Perhaps the most widely known German author is Johann Wolfgang von Goethe, who lived from 1749

to 1832. Goethe wrote novels, plays, and poetry. His most famous work is the dramatic poem *Faust.* In this play the aged scholar Faust is tempted by the devil Mephistopheles, but is finally victorious over him, thus showing that good can conquer evil. Some of Goethe's writing was done in Frankfurt am Main. Each year, people from many parts of the world come to visit his home here. Although the original house was destroyed in World War II, an exact replica stands in its place today.

Friedrich von Schiller, Goethe's close friend, also wrote plays and poems that have lived through the years. In Schiller's plays, the characters speak for freedom and the dignity of man. His play *William Tell* is the story of the struggle of the Swiss people to free themselves from the rule of tyrants.

Heinrich Heine, who lived from 1797 to 1856, is ranked among the greatest German lyric* poets. Heine's best poems are ballads, such as "The Lorelei" and "The Grenadiers." The collection of poetry that first helped to make him famous in Germany is *Book of Songs.* Many of Heine's ballads were set to music by German composers.

One of the most outstanding modern German writers was Thomas Mann. Many of Mann's novels and short stories compare the artist with the ordinary man. His first novel, *Buddenbrooks,* helped him to win the Nobel prize for literature, which is one of the greatest honors an author can receive. *The Magic Mountain,* a later book, is considered by many critics to be one of his most significant novels.

Gerhart Hauptmann, a well-known modern German dramatist who died in 1946, also won the Nobel prize for literature. Hauptmann wrote many realistic plays for the German theater. *The Weavers* is the best known of these plays. It has been produced many times in the United States.

German writers include a number of famous philosophers. In the eighteenth century, the philosopher Immanuel Kant wrote *Critique of Pure Reason,* in which he explored the limits of human knowledge. Another influential German philosopher was Georg Hegel. Hegel's *Encyclopedia of the Philosophical Sciences* and other works were later to help form the basis of Karl Marx's philosophy of communism. A third German philosopher, Friedrich Nietzsche, has had a

*See glossary

Thomas Mann (1875-1955) is considered to be one of Germany's most outstanding modern writers. German poets, novelists, and philosophers have contributed much to the world's store of literature.

great influence on writers and philosophers of the twentieth century. His writings criticized Christianity and developed the concept of superman, a man who directed all his efforts and passions into creative activity. The Nazis published parts of Nietzsche's writings to support their cause. However, their version of Nietzsche's philosophy was greatly distorted.

In addition to philosophical literature, the Germans have produced children's stories. Children in all parts of the world have heard or read "Snow White and the Seven Dwarfs," "Rumpelstiltskin," and "Hansel and Gretel." These tales were told around German firesides hundreds of years ago. In the early 1800's, two brothers, Jacob and Wilhelm Grimm, traveled through the countryside listening to these folktales. The brothers wrote down these tales and published them in book form. Today, the best of these tales are collected in a book called *Grimm's Fairy Tales*.

Composers. The music of German composers is perhaps Germany's greatest contribution to the arts of the Western world. Today, choirs still sing the chorales of Johann Sebastian Bach, and organists and pianists play works by this same composer. The symphonies of Ludwig van Beethoven are familiar to people in many parts of the world. Bach and Beethoven are only two of the great German composers. Others include Felix

A scene from "Die Meistersinger," an opera by Richard Wagner (1813-1883). The music of German composers is one of Germany's most outstanding contributions to the arts of the Western world.

A portrait of a merchant by Hans Holbein the Younger (1497?-1543). Hans Holbein the Younger, one of Germany's best-known artists, is ranked among the world's great portrait painters. His father, Hans Holbein the Elder, is best known for altar paintings of Jesus and Mary.

Mendelssohn, Robert Schumann, George Frederick Handel, Johannes Brahms, Richard Wagner, and Paul Hindemith.

Painters. Germany has also produced many master painters. One was the artist Albrecht Dürer, whose genius is seen in his engravings and woodcuts as well as in his paintings. Two other famous German artists were Hans Holbein the Elder and his son Hans Holbein the

Younger. The elder Holbein is best known for his beautiful altar paintings of Christ and Mary. The younger Holbein is ranked among the world's great portrait painters, although his religious paintings are also well known. (See picture above.)

German artists today. Present-day German painters, composers, and writers are not as well known as those of the past. This can be partly explained by the recent history of Germany. During the years that Hitler was in power, there was little freedom of thought, and it was very difficult for artists to create worthwhile works of art. (See Chapter 5.) Some German artists, such as Thomas Mann, left Germany and went to other countries. When Hitler's government ordered the imprisonment and death of German Jews, many brilliant artists in Germany perished in the gas chambers and concentration camps of Hitler's Germany.

Since World War II, freedom of thought has been restored in West Germany, but not in East Germany. The East German Communist leaders do not permit people to criticize their government. East German artists are expected to create works that encourage people to support the government. Artists who do not cooperate with the Communists may be asked to change what they have done. Restrictions such as these have caused many East German artists to flee to West Germany, where they are allowed to work in freedom.

Increasing Your Understanding

Studying about the arts and artists of a country can lead to a deeper understanding of that country and its history. As a class, make a study of the lives of some German artists and the periods of history in which they lived. You may want to divide into committees, with each committee studying one of the following artists:

Johann Sebastian Bach
Ludwig van Beethoven
Jacob and Wilhelm Grimm
Thomas Mann
Friedrich von Schiller

The suggestions on pages 178 and 179 will be helpful to you in locating information. When each committee has finished its research, a report of the study may be presented to the rest of the class. You may want to include the following in your report:

1. a brief biography of the artist
2. relationships between the work of the artist and the age in which he lived — give an example
3. examples of the artist's work such as photographs of his paintings, records of his music, or selections from his writings

The suggestions on page 183 will help your committee to work together successfully.

Sharing Ideas About Art

Think carefully about the following questions, and discuss them with your class:

1. Why shouldn't a government place restrictions on its artists?
2. What can you learn about a country by studying its art?

The suggestions on page 184 will help you have a successful class discussion.

Learning More About German Artists

One good way to learn about German painters is to examine and study photographs and prints of their paintings. With the help of your art teacher, find photographs and prints of the works of German artists. Then make an attractive art display in your classroom. Write a descriptive caption for each work, telling when it was painted and who the artist is. The suggestions on pages 178 and 179 will help you to locate information.

Reading Suggestions

Wheeler, Opal, and Deucher, Sybil. *Sebastian Bach*. New York: E.P. Dutton & Company, Inc., 1937.

Wheeler, Opal. *Ludwig Beethoven and the Chiming Tower Bells*. New York: E. P. Dutton & Company, Inc., 1942.

A resort area in Bavaria, West Germany. The people of West Germany love the out-of-doors and are very interested in the physical benefits of exercise.

19 Sports and Recreation

A Study Guide

Thoughts To Help You

Much can be learned about a country by seeing how its people spend their leisure time. As you study this chapter, see what recreation in Germany shows you about the following:

1. the type of countryside found in Germany
2. the climate in Germany
3. the history of Germany

The way the Germans spend their leisure time tells a great deal about the kind of people they are and the kind of society they have developed. Few people spend as much effort and money in organizing their leisure-time activities. At the same time, few people show more enthusiasm for simple pastimes such as group singing, or hiking in the countryside.

163

Although leisure-time activities in East and West Germany are very similar, they are carried on under very different conditions. Therefore, they are discussed separately in this chapter.

Athletic activities in West Germany. People in West Germany spend much of their time enjoying athletic activities. The West Germans like the out-of-doors, and they are very interested in the physical benefits of exercise. Sports clubs have been organized throughout the country, even in the smallest villages. Many of the nation's athletic activities are organized by the German Sports Federation. This organization is not controlled by the government.

West Germans take part in a variety of group sports. The most popular of these is soccer, which the Germans call football. Among the other athletic activities enjoyed in West Germany are group calisthenics. These group exercises require close teamwork, and are often performed at athletic festivals. One of the largest of these festivals is the Federal Youth Games, in which more than five million students take part throughout West Germany. Any boy or girl who performs well in five different

Soccer, which the Germans call football, is the most popular group sport in West Germany. Many West Germans who take part in athletic activities are members of sports clubs.

sports during the games receives the German Sports Badge.

The beautiful West German countryside, with its mountains, lakes, and rivers, encourages other types of athletic activities. In summer, many people set out with packs on their backs to camp in the open and to cook over campfires. If they wish, these hikers may sleep at night in large, rustic cabins called youth hostels, which have been built in the camping areas. Water sports such as sailing, boat racing, and swimming also are enjoyed by many people in West Germany.

Conditions for winter sports are also ideal in parts of West Germany. On weekends, trains and buses are crowded with thousands of skiers traveling to resorts in the mountains. One of the most famous ski resorts is Garmisch-Partenkirchen, high in the Alps. An Olympic ice stadium and bobsled run have been built at Garmisch. Some of the world's best skiers, skaters, and bobsledders come here for the International Sports Week that is held each year in January.

Musical activities in West Germany. In addition to sports, West Germans enjoy musical activities in their leisure time. Germany's history helps to explain why. During the centuries before Germany was united, in 1871, music and other forms of art were encouraged by the princely courts of the individual states. This gave people in many different parts of the country an opportunity to take part in cultural activities. Today, West Germany has about sixty permanent opera companies as well as many other musical groups. Even smaller towns have their own choral groups, and whenever possible, a band or an orchestra. In

Skiers in the Alps. On weekends, buses and trains in West Germany are crowded with skiers traveling to resorts in the mountains.

addition, music festivals are held in various parts of the country.

West Germans also enjoy lighter forms of music. There are concert gardens in West Germany in which small tables are placed in an open square surrounded by leafy trees. Here people listen to music as they eat and relax. Many of the young people in West Germany enjoy listening to American jazz, and some have formed their own jazz bands.

Plays and motion pictures in West Germany. The encouragement that the early princely courts of Germany gave to culture also helped people to take an interest in plays. Today, West Germany has about 60 private theaters and about

The Passion Play of Oberammergau attracts spectators from all over the world. It is presented every ten years by the people of this village.

120 theaters that are supported by local, state, or federal government funds. Some theaters in West Germany have one group of actors and actresses that act in many different plays during the year. Other theaters welcome touring companies that put on a single play for several weeks and then move on to a theater in another city. In this way, many people are able to see fine plays.

Many of the plays being produced in West Germany were written by foreign playwrights. Some of these are Americans, such as Tennessee Williams and Arthur Miller. Plays written by German dramatists are also being produced.

One of West Germany's most famous dramatic productions is the Oberammergau Passion Play, which tells the story of Christ's last days on earth. It is presented every ten years by the people of the village of Oberammergau, and attracts spectators from all over the world.

In addition to enjoying stage plays, the Germans like to attend motion pictures. Many motion-picture theaters have special afternoon showings for young people. About eight tenths of the films being shown today in West Germany were made in foreign countries. One of the main reasons West Germany does not produce more of its own films is that the principal prewar studios in Berlin were in the eastern part of the city. As a result, they were taken over by the Communists after the city was divided.

Festivals in West Germany. The good nature of the German people shows itself particularly at festival time. Festivals in West Germany are a time of singing, dancing, and laughter. These gay celebrations take place several times during the year. In the spring, there are carnivals, maypole dances, and colorful flower fairs. In the fall, there are wine festivals. The grandest of all festivals is the *Oktoberfest,* held in Munich each fall. This festival began in 1810 on the wedding day of King Ludwig I, and has been a time of fun and merrymaking ever since. During *Oktoberfest,* gay crowds of people dressed in festival costumes gather at the fairground to watch horseback-riding tournaments and to join in the dancing and singing. Huge festival tents are set up, where people enjoy the excellent sausages and Bavarian beer for which Germany is famous.

Leisure-time activities in East Germany. East Germans spend their leisure time in much the same way as West Germans. However, leisure-time activities in East Germany are mainly controlled by the government. The easiest way for young people in East Germany to take part in sports activities is to belong to the government-controlled Free German Youth. About two million of East Germany's young people are members of this organization. The Free German Youth trains its members to support the Communist government. It also tries to win their support by providing them with special privileges such as inexpensive holidays at the best beaches.

A youth festival in East Berlin. About two million of East Germany's young people belong to the government-controlled organization called the Free German Youth.

A flower festival in East Germany. Leisure-time activities in East Germany are similar to those in West Germany, but are largely under government control.

Cultural activities in East Germany are also controlled by the government. The government encourages only the kind of art that praises communism and inspires people to work for the state. All forms of art that disagree with the teachings of communism are frowned upon.

Checking Your Understanding

Write a paragraph for each of the topic sentences below. In each paragraph, expand and explain the idea in the topic sentence.

1. The land and climate of Germany enable the German people to enjoy many winter and summer sports.
2. Cultural activities occupy much of the German people's leisure time.
3. Many East German young people belong to the government-controlled Free German Youth organization.

The suggestions on pages 181 and 182 will help you to prepare a good paragraph.

Learning More About German Festivals

Imagine you have been sent to Germany as a newspaper reporter. Choose one of the following events and write an article about it for your newspaper:

1. Oberammergau Passion Play
2. *Oktoberfest* in Munich
3. International Sports Week at Garmisch-Partenkirchen

Try to make your article exciting and descriptive. Use this book and other sources to find information you need. Refer to the suggestions on pages 178-182 to help you find and evaluate information and to organize your material.

Learning About Maps

The earth is a sphere. Our earth is round like a ball. We call any object with this shape a sphere. The earth is, of course, a very large sphere. Its diameter* is about 8,000 miles. Its circumference* is about 25,000 miles. The earth is not quite a perfect sphere, however, for it is slightly flattened at the North and South poles.

Globes and maps. The globe in your classroom is also a sphere. It is a model of the earth. The surface of the globe shows the shapes of all the landmasses and bodies of water on the earth. By looking at the globe, you can see exactly where the continents, islands, and oceans are located. Globes are usually tilted to represent the way the earth is tilted.

Maps are flat drawings that represent part or all of the earth's surface. For example, the map on page 72 shows the city of Berlin. This map represents only a few square miles of the earth's surface. The map on pages 132 and 133, however, represents the world.

*See glossary

Scale. Globes and maps give information about distance. When you use them, you need to know how many miles on the earth are represented by a given distance on the globe or map. This relationship is called the scale. The scale of a globe or map may be expressed in several different ways.

On most maps, the scale is shown by a small drawing. For example:

Scale of Miles
0   200   400

Sometimes, the scale is expressed in this way: 1 inch = 400 miles.

Scale is often shown in another way, especially on globes and large maps. For example: 1:10,000,000. These numbers mean that any given distance on the globe or map represents a distance on the earth that is ten million times as large. When the scale is shown in this way, you may use any kind of measuring unit you wish. If you choose the inch, then one inch on the globe or map equals ten million inches on the earth, or about 158 miles. You might, however, prefer to use the centimeter,* another measuring unit. In that case, one centimeter on the globe or map would represent ten million centimeters on the earth, or 100 kilometers.

The San Francisco Bay area is a different size on each of the four maps below. This is because one inch on each of these maps represents a different distance on the earth. In other words, the scale of each of these maps is different.

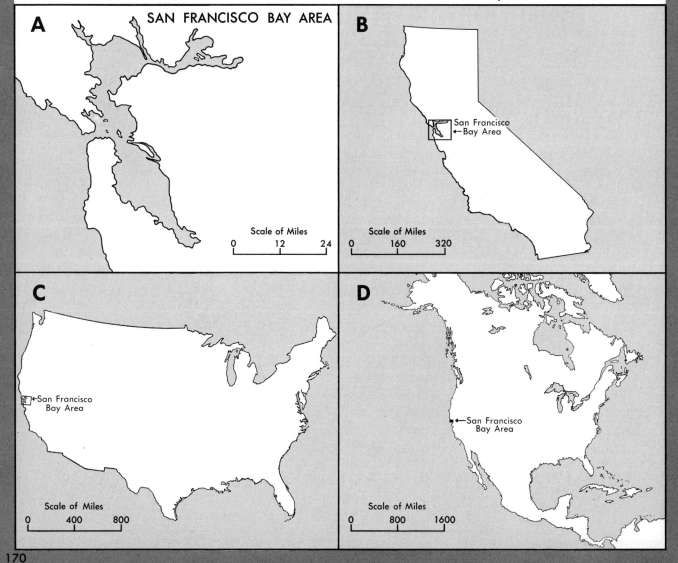

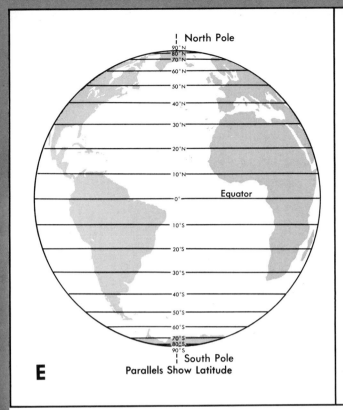

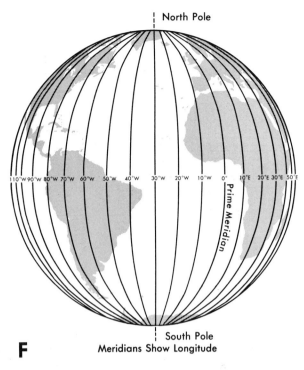

E
North Pole
Equator
South Pole
Parallels Show Latitude

F
North Pole
Prime Meridian
South Pole
Meridians Show Longitude

Locating places on the earth. Map makers, travelers, and other curious people have always wanted to know just where certain places are located. Over the years, a very accurate way of giving such information has been worked out. This system is used all over the world.

In order to work out a system for locating anything, you need starting points and a measuring unit. The North and South poles and the equator are the starting points for the system we use to locate places on the earth. The measuring unit for our system is called the degree (°).

Parallels show latitude. When we want to locate a place on the earth, we first find out how far it is north or south of the equator. This distance measured in degrees is called north or south latitude. The equator represents zero latitude. The North Pole is located at 90 degrees north latitude, and the South Pole is at 90 degrees south latitude.

All points on the earth that have the same latitude are the same distance from the equator. A line connecting such points is called a parallel. This is because it is parallel to the equator. (See illustration E, above.)

Meridians show longitude. After we know the latitude of a place, we need to know its location in an east-west direction. This is called its longitude. The lines that show longitude are called meridians. They are drawn so as to connect the North and South poles. (See illustration F, above.) Longitude is measured from the meridian that passes through Greenwich, England. This line of zero longitude is called the prime meridian. Distance east or west of this meridian measured in degrees is called east or west longitude.

Locating places on a globe. The location of a certain place might be given to you like this: 30°N 90°W. This means that this place is located 30 degrees north of the equator, and 90 degrees west of the prime meridian. See if you can find this place on the globe in your classroom. It is helpful to remember that parallels and meridians are drawn every ten or fifteen degrees on most globes.

The round earth on a flat map. An important fact about a sphere is that you cannot flatten out its surface perfectly. To prove this, you might perform an experiment. Cut an orange in half and scrape away the fruit.

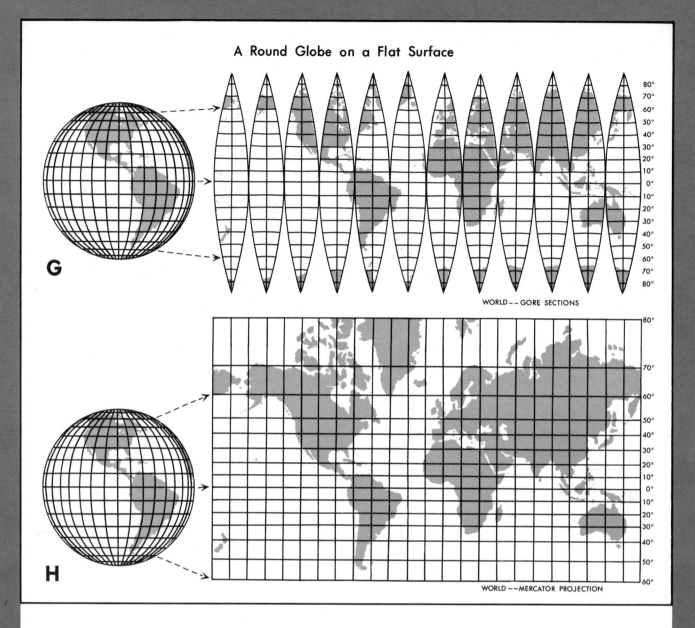

WORLD -- GORE SECTIONS

WORLD -- MERCATOR PROJECTION

You will not be able to press either piece of orange peel flat without crushing it. If you cut one piece in half, however, you can press these smaller pieces nearly flat. Next, cut one of these pieces of peel into three sections, or gores, shaped like those in illustration G, above. You will be able to press these small sections quite flat.

A map like the one shown in illustration G can be made by cutting the surface of a globe into twelve pieces shaped like the smallest sections of your orange peel. Such a map would be fairly accurate. However, an "orange-peel" map is not an easy map to use, because the continents and oceans are split apart.

A flat map can never show the earth's surface as truthfully as a globe can. On globes, shape, size, distance, and direction are all accurate. Although a single flat map of the world cannot be drawn to show all four of these things correctly, flat maps can be made that show some of these things accurately. The various ways of drawing maps of the world to show different things correctly are called map projections.

The Mercator* **projection.** Illustration H, above, shows a world map called a Mercator projection. When you compare this map with a globe, you can see that continents, islands, and oceans have almost the right shape. On this kind of map, however, North America seems larger than Africa, which is not true. On Mercator maps, lands far from the equator appear larger than they are.

Because they show true directions, Mercator maps are especially useful to navigators. For instance, the city of Lisbon, Portugal, lies almost exactly east of Baltimore, Maryland. A Mercator map shows that a ship could reach Lisbon by sailing from Baltimore straight east across the Atlantic Ocean.

The shortest route. Strangely enough, the best way to reach Lisbon from Baltimore is not by traveling straight east. There is a shorter route. In order to understand why this is so, you might like to perform the following experiment.

On your classroom globe, locate Lisbon and Baltimore. Both cities lie just south of the 40th parallel. Take a piece of string and connect the two cities. Let the string follow the true east-west direction of the 40th parallel. Now, draw the string tight. Notice that it passes far to the north of the 40th parallel. The path of the tightened string is the shortest route between Baltimore and Lisbon. The shortest route between any two points on the earth is called the great* circle route.

The gnomonic (nō mon′ ik) **projection.** Using a globe and a piece of string is not a very handy or accurate way of finding great circle routes. Instead, sailors and fliers use a special kind of map called the gnomonic projection. (See illustration I, below.) On this kind of map, the great circle route between any two places can be found simply by drawing a straight line between them.

Equal-area projections. Mercator and gnomonic maps are both very useful, but they do not show true areas. They cannot be used when you want to compare areas in different parts of the world. This is because sections of these maps that are the same size do not always represent the same amounts of the earth's surface.

Maps that do show true areas are called equal-area projections. If one square* inch of such a map represents a certain number of square miles on the earth's surface, then every other square inch of the map will represent an equal number of square miles on the earth. In order to draw an equal-area map of the world on a flat surface, the shapes of the landmasses and bodies of water must be distorted. (See illustration J, below.) To avoid this, some equal-area maps are broken, or interrupted. The breaks are arranged to fall at places that are not important. (See illustration K, below.)

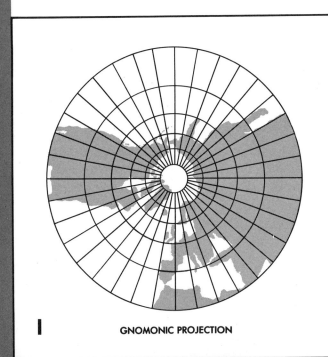

I   GNOMONIC PROJECTION

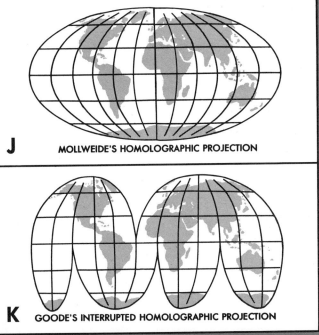

J   MOLLWEIDE'S HOMOLOGRAPHIC PROJECTION

K   GOODE'S INTERRUPTED HOMOLOGRAPHIC PROJECTION

SPECIAL-PURPOSE MAPS

Maps that show part of the earth. For some purposes, we prefer maps that do not show the entire surface of the earth. A map of a very small area can be drawn more accurately than a map of a large area. It can also include more details.

Illustration L, below, shows a photograph and a map of the same small part of the earth. The drawings on the map that show the shape and location of things on the earth are called symbols. The small drawing that shows directions is called a compass* rose.

Maps for special purposes. Maps can show the location of many different kinds of things. For instance, a map can show what minerals are found in certain places, or what crops are grown. A small chart that lists the symbols and their meanings is usually included on a map. This is called the legend, or key. (See map N, below.)

Symbols on some geography maps stand for the amounts of things in different places. For instance, map M, below, gives information about the number of people in the western part of the United States. The key tells the meaning of the symbols, which in this case are dots and circles.

There are other ways of giving information about quantity on maps. For example, a rainfall map is shown on page 28. On this map, various designs, or patterns, are used to indicate the areas of Europe that receive different amounts of rainfall each year.

Maps also help us to understand events that have happened in history. Changes in German history are shown on the maps on pages 38, 41, 45, 48, 56, and 86.

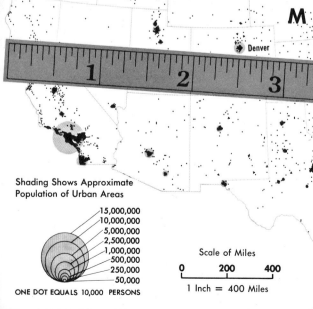

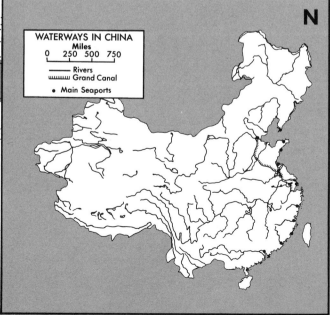

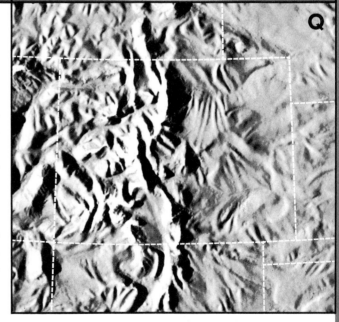

RELIEF MAPS

Some globes and maps show the roughness of the earth's surface. From a jet plane, you can see that the earth's surface is irregular. You can see mountains and valleys, hills and plains. For some purposes, globes and maps that show these things are needed. They are called relief globes and maps.

Since globes are three-dimensional models of the earth, you may wonder why most globes do not show the roughness of the earth's surface. The reason for this is that the highest mountain on the earth is not very large when it is compared with the earth's diameter. Even a very large globe would be almost perfectly smooth.

In order to make a relief globe or map, you must use a different scale for the height of the land. For example, you might start with a large flat map. One inch on your flat map represents a distance of one hundred miles on the earth. Now you are going to make a model of a mountain on your map. On the earth, this mountain is two miles high. If you let one inch represent a height of two miles on the earth, your mountain should rise one inch above the flat surface of

your map. Other mountains and hills should be modeled on this same scale.

By photographing relief globes and maps, flat maps can be made that show the earth much as it looks from an airplane. Maps O and P, at the top of this page, are photographs of a relief globe. Map Q is a photograph of a relief map.

Topographic maps. Another kind of map that shows the roughness of the earth's surface is called a topographic, or contour, map. On this kind of map, lines are drawn to show

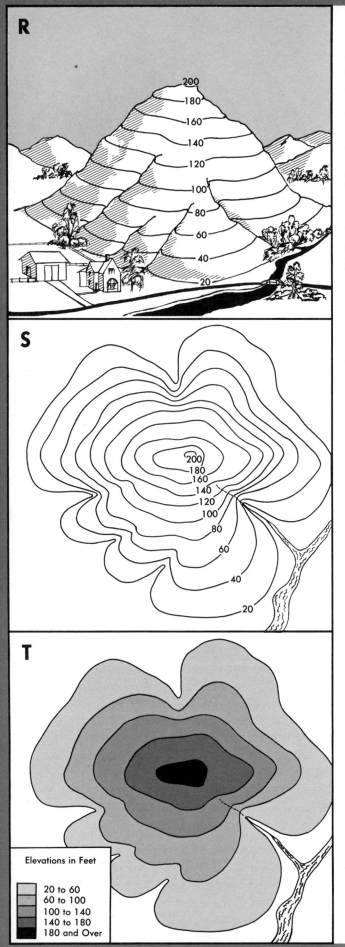

different heights of the earth's surface. These are called contour lines. The illustrations on this page help to explain how topographic maps are made.

Illustration R is a drawing of a hill. Around the bottom of the hill is our first contour line. This line connects all the points at the base of the hill that are exactly twenty feet above sea level. Higher up the hill, another contour line is drawn, connecting all the points that are exactly forty feet above sea level. A line is also drawn at a height of sixty feet. Other lines are drawn every twenty feet until the top of the hill is reached. Since the hill is shaped somewhat like a cone, each contour line is shorter than the one just below it.

Illustration S shows how the contour lines in the drawing of the hill (R) can be used to make a topographic map. This map gives us a great deal of information about the hill. Since each line is labeled with the height it represents, you can tell how high the different parts of the hill are. It is important to remember that land does not really rise in layers, as you might think when you look at a topographic map. Wherever the contour lines are far apart, you can be sure that the land slopes gently. Where they are close together, the slope is steep. With practice, you can picture the land in your mind as you look at such a map. Topographic maps are especially useful to men who design such things as roads and buildings.

On a topographic map, the spaces between the contour lines may be filled in with different shades of gray. If a different shade of gray were used for each different height of land shown in map S, there would be ten shades. It would be very hard for you to tell these different shades of gray apart. Therefore on map T, at left, black and four shades of gray were used to show differences in height of forty feet. The key box shows the height of the land represented by the different shades. On some topographic maps, colors are used to represent different heights of land.

SOCIAL STUDIES SKILLS

What is a skill? A skill is something that you have learned to do well. To learn some skills, such as swimming, you must train the muscles of your arms and legs. To learn others, such as typing, you must train your fingers. Still other skills require you to train your mind. For example, reading with understanding is a skill that requires much mental training.

Why are skills important? Mastering different skills will help you to have a more satisfying life. You will be healthier and enjoy your leisure time more if you develop skills needed to take part in various sports. By developing artistic skills, you will be able to express your feelings more fully. It is even more important for you to develop skills of the mind. These skills are the tools that you will use in obtaining and using the knowledge you need to live successfully in today's world.

To develop a skill, you must practice it correctly. If you ask a fine athlete or musician how he gained his skill, he will say, "Through practice." To develop skills of the mind, you must practice also. Remember, however, that a person cannot become a good ballplayer if he keeps throwing the ball incorrectly. The same thing is true of mental skills. To master them, you must practice them correctly.

The following pages contain suggestions about how to perform correctly several important skills needed in the social studies. Study these skills carefully, and use them.

HOW TO FIND INFORMATION YOU NEED

Knowing how to find information is a skill that you will use throughout your life.

Each day of your life you seek information. Sometimes you want to know certain facts just because you are curious. Most of the time, however, you want information for some special purpose. If your hobby is baseball, for example, you may want to know how to figure batting averages. If you collect stamps, you need to know how to identify the countries they come from. As a student in today's world, you need information for many purposes. As an adult, you will need even more knowledge in order to live successfully in tomorrow's world.

You may wonder how you can possibly learn all the facts you are going to need during your lifetime. The answer is that you can't. Therefore, knowing where to find information when you need it is of vital importance to you. Below are suggestions for locating good sources of information and for using these sources to find the facts that you need.

Written Sources of Information

1. <u>Books</u>. You may be able to find the information you need in books that you have at home or in your classroom. To see if a textbook or other nonfiction book has the information you need, look at the table of contents and the index.

Sometimes, you will need to go to your school or community library to locate books that contain the information you want. To make the best use of a library, you should learn to use the card catalog. This is a file that contains information about the books in the library. Each nonfiction book has at least three cards, filed in alphabetical order. One is for the title, one is for the author, and one is for the subject of the book. Each card gives the book's special number. This number will help you to find the book, since all the nonfiction books in the library are arranged on the shelves in numerical order. If you cannot find a book you want, the librarian will be glad to help you.

2. <u>Reference volumes</u>. You will find much useful information in special books known as reference volumes. These include dictionaries, encyclopedias, atlases, and other special books. Some companies publish a book each year with statistics and general information about the events of the preceding year. Such books are usually called yearbooks, annuals, or almanacs.

3. <u>Newspapers and magazines</u>. These are an important source of up-to-date information. Sometimes you will want to look for information in papers or magazines that you do not have at home. You can usually find the ones you want at the library.

The *Readers' Guide to Periodical Literature,* which is available in most libraries, will direct you to magazine articles about the subject you are investigating. This is a series of volumes that list articles by title, author, and subject. In the front of each volume is an explanation of the abbreviations used to indicate the different magazines and their dates.

4. <u>Booklets, pamphlets, and bulletins</u>. Many materials of this type are available from local and state governments, as well as from our federal government. Chambers of commerce, travel bureaus, trade organizations, private companies, and embassies

of foreign countries publish materials that contain a wealth of information.

Many booklets and bulletins give accurate information. You should remember, however, that some of them are intended to promote certain products or ideas. Information obtained from such sources should be checked carefully.

Other Ways of Obtaining Information

1. Direct experience. What you observe or experience for yourself may be a good source of information if you have observed carefully and remembered accurately. Firsthand information can often be obtained by visiting places in your community or nearby, such as museums, factories, or government offices.

2. Radio and television. Use the listings in your local newspaper to find programs about the subjects in which you are interested.

3. Movies, filmstrips, recordings, and slides. Materials on a great variety of subjects are available. They can be obtained from schools, libraries, museums, and private companies.

4. Resource people. Sometimes, you will be able to obtain information by interviewing a person who has special knowledge. On occasion, you may wish to invite someone to speak to your class and answer questions.

EVALUATING INFORMATION

During your lifetime, you will constantly need to evaluate what you see, hear, and read. Information is not true or significant simply because it is presented on television or is written in a book, magazine, or newspaper. The following suggestions will help you in evaluating information.

Learn to tell the difference between primary and secondary sources of information. A primary source of information is a firsthand record. For example, a photograph taken of an event while it is happening is a primary source. So is the report you write about a field trip you take. Original docu-

ments, such as the Constitution of the United States, are primary sources, also.

A secondary source is a secondhand report. For example, if you write a report about what someone else told you he saw, your report will be a secondary source of information. Another example of a secondary source is a history book.

Advanced scholars like to use primary sources whenever possible. However, these sources are often difficult to obtain. Most students in elementary and high school use secondary sources. You should always be aware that you are using secondhand information when you use a secondary source.

Find out who said it and when it was said. The next step in evaluating information is to ask, "Who said it?" Was it a scholar with special training in the subject about which he wrote? Was it a newsman with a reputation for careful reporting of the facts?

Another question you should ask is, "When was it said?" Changes take place rapidly in our world, and the information you are using may be out of date. For example, many nations in Africa have won independence in recent years, so a political map of this continent that is five years old is no longer accurate.

Find out if it is mainly fact or opinion. The next step in evaluating information is to decide whether it is based on facts or whether it mainly consists of unsupported opinions. You can do this best if you are aware of these three types of statements:

1. Statements of fact that can be checked. For example, "Voters in the United States choose their representatives by secret ballot." This statement can be checked by observing how voting is carried on in different parts of our country.

2. Inferences, or conclusions that are based on facts. For example, "The people of the United States live in a democracy." This statement is based on the fact that citizens in the United States choose their representatives by secret ballot,

and on other facts that can be proved. It is important to remember that inferences can be false or only partly true.

3. Value judgments, or opinions. The statement, "It is wrong for some people to be forced to live in poverty," is a value judgment. Since a value judgment is an opinion, you need to examine it very critically. On what facts and inferences is it based? For example, what facts and conclusions do you think form the basis of the opinion, "It is wrong for people to be forced to live in poverty"? Do you agree with these conclusions? A reliable writer or reporter is careful to let his reader know which statements in his writing are his own opinions. He also tries to base his opinions as much as possible on facts that can be proved.

Find out why it was said. The next step in evaluating information is to find out the purpose for which it was prepared. Many books and articles are prepared in an honest effort to give you accurate information. For example, a scientist writing about a new scientific discovery will usually try to report his findings as accurately as possible, and he will be careful to distinguish between what he has actually observed and the conclusions he has drawn from these facts.

Some information, however, is prepared mainly to persuade people to believe or act a certain way. Information of this kind is called propaganda.

Some propaganda is used to promote causes that are generally considered good. A United States Army recruiting poster with a big picture of Uncle Sam and the words, "Uncle Sam needs *you*," is an example of this type of propaganda.

Propaganda is also used to make people support causes they would not agree with if they knew more about them. This kind of propaganda may consist of information that is true, partly true, or false. Even when it is true, however, the information may be presented in such a way as to mislead you.

Propaganda generally appeals to people's emotions rather than to their reasoning ability. For this reason, you should learn to identify information that is propaganda. Then you can think about it calmly and clearly, and evaluate it intelligently.

Seven Propaganda Tricks

People who use propaganda have learned many ways of presenting information to influence you in the direction they wish. Seven propaganda tricks to watch for are listed below.

Name Calling. Giving a label that is disliked or feared, such as "un-American," to an organization, a person, or an idea. This trick often persuades people to reject something they know nothing about.

Glittering Generalities. Trying to win support by using fine-sounding phrases, such as "the best deal in town" or "the American way." These phrases have no clear meaning when you stop and think about them.

Transfer. Connecting a person, product, or idea with something that people already feel strongly about. For example, displaying a picture of a church next to a speaker to give the impression that he is honest and trustworthy.

Testimonial. Getting well-known persons or organizations to announce in public their support of a person, product, or idea.

Plain Folks. Trying to win support by giving the impression of being just an ordinary person who can be trusted. For example, a political candidate may try to win people's confidence by giving the impression that he is a good father who loves children and dogs.

Card Stacking. Giving the wrong impression by giving only part of the facts about a person, product, or idea. For example, giving favorable facts and leaving out unfavorable ones.

Bandwagon. Trying to win support by saying that "everybody knows that" or "everyone is doing this."

Preparing a report will give you practice in the skills of organizing and presenting information.

MAKING REPORTS

There are many occasions when you need to share information or ideas with others. Sometimes you will need to do this in writing. Other times you will need to do it orally. One of the best ways to develop your writing and speaking skills is by making oral and written reports. The success of your report will depend on how well you have organized your material. It will also depend on your skill in presenting it. Here are some guidelines that will help you in preparing a good report.

Decide upon a goal. Have your purpose clearly in mind. Are you mainly interested in communicating information? Do you want to give your own viewpoint on a subject, or are you trying to persuade other people to agree with you?

Find sources of information. Be sure to use more than one source. If you are not sure where to find information about your topic, read the suggestions on pages 178 and 179.

Take good notes. To remember what you have read, you must take notes. Before you begin taking notes, however, you will need to make a list of the main ideas that you plan to include in your report. As you do research, you may need to add other ideas to your list. Write down the facts you find that help support these main ideas. Your notes should be brief and in your own words unless you want to use an exact quotation.

You will be able to make the best use of your notes if you write them on file cards. Use a separate card for each statement or group of statements that supports one of your main ideas. To remember where your information came from, write on each card the title, author, and date of the source.

When you have finished taking notes, evaluate the information on your cards. Group the cards according to your main ideas. This will help you arrange your material in logical order.

Make an outline. An outline is a general plan that shows the order and the relationship of ideas. The main ideas you have selected will serve as headings. (See example below.) Supporting ideas and facts are listed under the main headings. As you arrange your information, ask yourself the following questions:

a. Is there one main idea that I must put first because everything else depends on it?
b. Have I arranged my facts in such a way as to show relationships among them?
c. Are there some ideas that will be clearer if they are discussed after other ideas have been explained?
d. Have I included enough facts so that I can complete my outline with a summary statement or a logical conclusion?

When you have completed your first outline, you may find that some parts of it are skimpy. If so, you may wish to do more research. When you are satisfied that you have enough information, make your final outline. Remember that this outline will serve as the basis of your finished report.

Example of an outline. The author of this feature prepared the following outline before beginning to write.

Special guidelines for a written report. Using your outline as a guide, write your report. Remember to follow all of the rules for good writing that you have learned. It is usually best to begin a paragraph with a topic sentence that says to the reader, "This is what you will learn about in the paragraph." The other sentences in the paragraph should help to support or explain the topic sentence. The paragraphs in this book are good examples of clear writing. Use the dictionary to help you spell words you are doubtful about. With your report, include a list of the sources you used. This list is called a bibliography.

Special guidelines for an oral report. When you are going to give a report orally, you will also want to organize your information in a logical order by making an outline. Prepare notes to guide you during your talk. These notes should be complete enough to help you remember all the points you want to make. You may even write out certain portions of your report that you prefer to read.

When you present your report, speak directly to your audience. Pronounce your words correctly and distinctly. Remember to speak slowly enough for your listeners to follow what you are saying. Stand up straight, but try not to be too stiff. Remember, the only way to improve your speaking skills is to practice them correctly.

Working well with others is an important skill.

WORKING WITH OTHERS

In school and throughout life, you will find that there are many projects that can be done better by a group than by one person working alone. Some of these projects would take too long to finish if they were done by a single individual. Others have different parts that can be done best by people with different talents.

Before your group begins a project, you should decide several matters. First, determine exactly what you are trying to accomplish. Second, decide what part of the project each person should do. Third, schedule when the project is to be completed.

The group will do a better job and reach its goals more quickly if each person follows these suggestions:

1. Do your part. Remember that the success of your project depends on every member of the group. Be willing to do your share of the work and to accept your share of the responsibility.

2. Follow the rules. Help the group decide on sensible rules, and then follow them. When a difference of opinion cannot be settled by discussion, make a decision by majority vote.

3. Share your ideas. Be willing to share your ideas and talents with the group. When you submit an idea for discussion, be prepared to see it criticized or even rejected. At the same time, have the courage to stick up for a principle or a belief that is really important to you.

4. Respect others. Remember that every person is an individual with different beliefs and talents. Give the other members of the group a chance to be heard, and be ready to appreciate the work and ideas they contribute.

5. Be friendly, thoughtful, helpful, and cheerful. Try to express your opinions seriously and sincerely without hurting others or losing their respect. Listen politely to the ideas of others.

6. Learn from your mistakes. Look for ways in which you can be a better group member the next time you work with others on a project.

Share your ideas and appreciate the work of others.

HOLDING A GROUP DISCUSSION

One of the important ways in which you learn is by exchanging ideas with other people. You do this frequently in informal conversation. You are likely to learn more, however, when you take part in the special kind of group conversation that we call a discussion. A discussion is more orderly than a conversation, and it usually has a definite, serious purpose. This purpose may be the sharing of information or the solving of a problem. In order to reach its goal, the discussion group must arrive at a conclusion or make a decision of some kind.

A discussion is more likely to be successful when those who take part in it observe the following guidelines:

1. Be prepared. Think about the topic to be discussed ahead of time. Prepare for the discussion by reading and taking notes. You may also want to make an outline of the ideas you want to share with the group.

2. Take part. Contribute to the discussion; express your ideas clearly and concisely. Be sure that the statements you make and the questions you ask deal with the topic being discussed. This will help the discussion move along toward a successful conclusion.

3. Listen and think. Listen thoughtfully to others. Encourage all of the members of the discussion group to express their ideas. Do not make up your mind about a question or a problem until all of the facts have been given. Be ready to help the group summarize the information presented during the discussion.

4. Be courteous. When you speak, address the entire group. Ask and answer questions politely. When you disagree with someone, point out your reasons calmly and in a friendly way.

Taking part in a group discussion provides an opportunity to exchange ideas with others.

GLOSSARY
COMPLETE PRONUNCIATION KEY

The pronunciation of each word is shown just after the word, in this way: **gnomonic** (nō mon′ik). The letters and signs used are pronounced as in the words below. The mark ′ is placed after a syllable with primary or strong accent, as in the example above. The mark ′ after a syllable shows a secondary or lighter accent, as in **Zollverein** (tsôl′fer īn′).

Some words, taken from foreign languages, are spoken with sounds that otherwise do not occur in English. Symbols for these sounds are given at the end of the table as " foreign sounds."

a	hat, cap	j	jam, enjoy	u	cup, butter
ā	age, face	k	kind, seek	u̇	full, put
ã	care, air	l	land, coal	ü	rule, move
ä	father, far	m	me, am	ū	use, music
		n	no, in		
b	bad, rob	ng	long, bring		
ch	child, much			v	very, save
d	did, red	o	hot, rock	w	will, woman
		ō	open, go	y	young, yet
		ô	order, all	z	zero, breeze
e	let, best	oi	oil, voice	zh	measure, seizure
ē	equal, see	ou	house, out		
ėr	term, learn				
		p	paper, cup		
f	fat, if	r	run, try	ə	represents:
g	go, bag	s	say, yes	a	in about
h	he, how	sh	she, rush	e	in taken
		t	tell, it	i	in pencil
i	it, pin	th	thin, both	o	in lemon
ī	ice, five	℡H	then, smooth	u	in circus

foreign sounds

Y as in French *du*. Pronounce ē with the lips rounded as for English ü in rule.

œ as in French *peu*. Pronounce ā with the lips rounded as for ō.

N as in French *bon*. The N is not pronounced, but shows that the vowel before it is nasal.

H as in German *ach*. Pronounce k without closing the breath passage.

Allies. See **World War I** and **World War II**.

Alsace-Lorraine (al′sās lə rän′). A French region bounded on the north by Belgium, Luxembourg, and Germany, on the east by the Rhine River, and on the south by Switzerland. Alsace-Lorraine is an important agricultural and industrial region. Both French-speaking and German-speaking peoples live in Alsace-Lorraine. This region passed from France to Germany in 1871, was returned to France in 1919, annexed by Germany in 1940, and returned to France in 1945.

altitude. Height above the level of the sea. For example, a mountain that rises 10,000 feet above sea level has an altitude of 10,000 feet.

appreciation. An awareness or understanding of the worth or value of something. For example, you may develop an appreciation for music or art, or for the accomplishments of the people of a nation.

atomic energy. Energy that is stored in atoms. All matter is made up of tiny atoms, which are much too small to be seen. When atoms are split or combined in certain ways, great amounts of energy are released. This energy can be used for many purposes, including the production of electricity.

axis of the earth. An imaginary straight line that passes through the earth, joining the North and South poles. It takes the earth about twenty-four hours to rotate, or turn around, once on its axis.

Bach (bäH), **Johann Sebastian,** 1685-1750. A German musician and composer, born at Eisenach. After serving as a church organist and as a musical director for members of the nobility, Bach in 1723 became organist and choirmaster at Leipzig, a position he held until his death. His works include many types of instrumental music as well as works for choral use. Few of his compositions were published during his lifetime.

Beethoven (bā′tō vən), **Ludwig van,** 1770-1827. A German musician and composer who was born in Bonn. In 1792 he settled in Vienna to continue his musical education. Here he soon gained fame as a musician and composer. From 1798, Beethoven was troubled by growing deafness, but he continued to compose until his death. Among his compositions are symphonies, chamber music, and choral works.

bituminous coal. The most plentiful and important type of coal. Bituminous coal is used for making coke, the fuel used in smelting iron ore. It is also used to heat homes and factories.

Bohemia (bō hē′miə). A region of central Europe, comprising what is now the western part of Czechoslovakia. (See map, pages 10 and 11.) Once a powerful kingdom, Bohemia came under Austrian rule in 1526. It is the homeland of a Slavic people called the Czechs. See **Slavs.**

Brahms (brämz), **Johannes,** 1833-1897. A German composer, born in Hamburg. For many years, Brahms traveled in Europe as a pianist or occupied positions as choir director or conductor. Among his compositions are songs, symphonies, concertos, and chamber music. Brahms often is considered to be the last of the great classical composers.

Bundestag. One of the two national lawmaking assemblies of West Germany. (See pages 84 and 85.)

centimeter (sen′tə mē′tər). A unit for measuring length. It is equal to slightly less than one-half inch. The centimeter is a unit in the metric system of measurement. The metric system is used in most countries and by scientists throughout the world. In this system, 100 centimeters equal one meter, and 1000 meters equal one kilometer. A meter is about 39 inches in length, and a kilometer is equal to about two thirds of a mile.

circumference (sər kum′fər əns). The distance around a circle or a sphere.

city-state. An independent state made up of a city and the territory around it.

Cold War. The conflict between the democratic nations of the world and the Communist nations. It is called a cold war because it is fought largely with propaganda and with economic and social pressures rather than with guns.

collectivized farming. Refers to the combining of small farms to form large government-controlled farms.

commune (kom′ūn). A unit of local government in France, West Germany, and some other European countries. A commune is somewhat like a township in the United States.

communism. A system of society characterized by common ownership of property rather than private ownership. Although the idea of common ownership is very old, the terms communism and socialism, which are associated with this idea, did not come into use until the early part of the nineteenth century. These two terms were used more or less interchangeably at first. Fundamental to communism, however, was the belief that violent revolution was the only way to bring productive property under common control. Socialism was associated more with peaceful, legal methods of achieving this goal. See **socialism.** In the twentieth century, the term communism has become associated with the beliefs and actions of the Communist parties of the Soviet Union and other countries. Members of these parties believe that Communist governments must be established throughout the world. Under a Communist government, there is no individual liberty. Industry, farming, trade, transportation, communication, education, and most other activities are controlled by the government. Because a Communist government virtually controls its citizens' lives, it is called a totalitarian dictatorship.

compass rose. A small drawing included on a map to show directions. A compass rose is often used as a decoration. Here are three examples of compass roses:

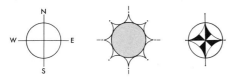

concept. The idea behind a word or a phrase. A concept is general rather than specific. For example, the word "river" does not refer to one particular river. Instead, it expresses the idea of any large, natural-flowing stream of water.

cooperative. An economic organization formed for the mutual benefit of its members. In Communist East Germany, farmers have been pressured into joining agricultural-producers' cooperatives. These cooperatives are run in accordance with the national economic plan and must deliver part of their harvest to the government at fixed prices. The farmers are organized into brigades. They are assigned specific work and are directed by the managing committee of their cooperative.

depression. In industrialized societies, a period when there is relatively little business activity and many people are unemployed.

diameter (dī am′ ə tər). The length of a straight line that extends from one side of a circle or a sphere to the other. This line must pass through the exact center of the circle or sphere.

dictatorship. A government in which all ruling power is held by a single leader or by a small group of leaders.

equator (i kwā′tər). An imaginary line around the middle of the earth. It divides the earth into a northern half and a southern half.

equinox. The time when the sun shines directly on the equator. This happens twice during the year. The spring equinox is about March 21. The autumn equinox is about September 22. On these dates, night and day are the same length everywhere on earth.

Eurasia (ūr ā'zhə). The largest landmass on the earth, composed of Europe and Asia.

generalization. A general statement showing a relationship between two or more concepts. See **concept**. The following statement is an example of a generalization: A country's industries depend on raw materials, transportation, and the skill of its people.

gnomonic (nō mon'ik) **projection.** A map projection made on a plane surface tangent to a globe, with the light source at the center of the globe. A map drawn on this projection cannot include an entire hemisphere, and it does not show shapes, areas, or directions accurately. Such a map is useful to navigators, however, because any straight line drawn on it lies on a great circle. A navigator draws a straight line on the map, connecting the beginning and end points of his trip. He then selects places along this line, and determines the latitude and longitude of these points. Next, he marks these points on a Mercator map, and connects them with straight lines. The straight lines on the Mercator map give him true directions. With these, he can set his compass and steer a course that lies approximately on the great circle route for his journey.

Goethe (gœ'tə), **Johann Wolfgang von,** 1749-1832. Germany's greatest poet, Goethe was born in Frankfurt am Main.

great circle. Any imaginary circle around the earth that divides its surface exactly in half. The equator, for example, is a great circle. The shortest route between any two points on the earth always lies on a great circle.

Great Depression. The depression that began in the United States in 1929 and had worldwide effects. See **depression**. World trade declined, and many nations faced severe economic crises.

Handel, George Frederick, 1685-1759. A composer and musical director, born in Halle, Germany. In 1706 Handel went to Italy, where he learned new forms and techniques from his musical surroundings. Several years later he went to England. Here Handel spent most of his life as a composer and producer of operas and oratorios. *The Messiah* is one of his many religious oratorios.

Hauptmann, Gerhart, 1862-1946. A German writer, born in Obersalzbrunn, Silesia.

Hegel (hā'gəl), **Georg Wilhelm Friedrich,** 1770-1831. A German philosopher whose ideas strongly influenced a number of other philosophers, including Karl Marx. See **Marx, Karl**. Hegel was born in Stuttgart. He received his education in the field of theology and served much of his adult life as a university professor. Among his writings are works on philosophy, history, and religion.

Heine, Heinrich, 1797-1856. German writer of poetry and prose, born in Düsseldorf. Heine was the son of a businessman and worked both in business and law before turning to history and literature. Highly interested in liberal ideas, he migrated to Paris in 1831, where he accepted a pension from the French government and worked as a revolutionary journalist. Heine's poetry is characterized by its simplicity and has many aspects of the folk song. Many of Heine's poems have been set to music.

hemisphere. Half of a sphere. In the study of geography, the earth may be divided at the equator into the Northern Hemisphere and the Southern Hemisphere.

Hindemith, Paul, 1895-1963. A German musician and composer who was born at Hanau and studied music in Frankfurt am Main, where he later became conductor of the opera. The Nazis banned his works in 1933. In 1939, he emigrated to the United States, where he became an American citizen and an instructor in music at Yale University. From 1953 until his death, Hindemith made his home in Switzerland. Among Hindemith's compositions are operas, chamber music, and choral works.

Hindenburg, Paul von, 1847-1934. A general in World War I who took command of all the German armies in 1916. In 1925 he was elected president of the German Republic, but he believed in monarchy and did not understand the problems he faced. Hindenburg permitted the presidency to become weak. He appointed chancellors and permitted them more and more power. In 1932 he was reelected president, defeating Hitler. In 1933, however, his advisors persuaded him to appoint Hitler as chancellor. When von Hindenburg died, Hitler became ruler of Germany.

Holbein, Hans, the Elder, 1465?-1524. A German artist who was born at Augsburg. There are no records of his early life, but by 1493 he was a painter in Augsburg. Most of Holbein's art was religious. He painted many altarpieces in German cities. Among his other works are designs for glass windows and portraits. Holbein is known for rich colors and the individualization of his subjects.

Holbein, Hans, the Younger, 1497?-1543. A German artist, the son of Hans Holbein the Elder. See **Holbein, Hans,** the Elder. He was born at Augsburg and received his early training from his father. Later he studied in Switzerland, and settled in the city of Basel. He traveled and worked in France, the Netherlands, England, and Italy. Holbein is famous for his portraits and drawings, and for his series of woodcuts called "The Dance of Death."

hydroelectric. Refers to electricity produced by waterpower. The force of rushing water runs machines, called generators, that produce electricity.

hypotheses (hī poth′i sēz). Possible solutions, or "educated guesses." A hypothesis may prove to be false, but it helps us in our search for the right solution to a problem.

Ice Age. A period in the earth's history during which great masses of ice repeatedly covered much of the land in the Northern Hemisphere. These masses of ice, which were from 5,000 to 10,000 feet thick, advanced and retreated four times. Between these times of glaciation, the climate in the affected areas was as warm as or perhaps warmer than at present, so that plant and animal life reestablished itself during these interglacial times. It is believed that the Ice Age lasted about one million years, and that the last retreat of the ice mass occurred about eleven thousand years ago.

indulgence. In the Roman Catholic Church, a remission, or pardon, of temporal punishment for sin. The Church teaches that a sinner is not only guilty but also owes a debt of punishment. Forgiveness of the guilt does not take away the debt of punishment. By obtaining an indulgence, the sinner has part or all of his debt of temporal punishment taken away. This debt is paid from the spiritual treasury accumulated by the merits of Christ and the good works of the saints. During the Middle Ages, the payment of money, to be used for religious purposes, was

---

PRONUNCIATION KEY: hat, āge, cãre, fär; let, ēqual, tèrm; it, īce; hot, ōpen, ôrder; oil, out; cup, pùt, rüle, ūse; child; long; thin; ŧHen; zh, measure; ə represents a in about, e in taken, i in pencil, o in lemon, u in circus. For the complete key, see page 185.

permitted as one of the conditions for obtaining some indulgences. Serious abuses arose because of this, especially when some persons came to regard indulgences as a substitute for sorrow and confession of their sins.

Iron Curtain. Refers to the barrier of secrecy and censorship that divides the Communist and non-Communist nations of Europe.

Kant, Immanuel, 1724-1804. A German philosopher who greatly influenced modern philosophy, born in Königsberg.

liberal. Refers to the beliefs of liberals. See **liberals.**

liberals. In the eighteenth and nineteenth centuries, the term generally was used in connection with people who sought as much freedom as possible for the individual from restrictions imposed by institutions, such as government and church. Liberals today also place great emphasis on the freedom of the individual, but they no longer consider government to be an enemy. Rather, they look to government as an instrument to help better the condition of man.

loess (lō'is). A type of fertile, dustlike soil. Scientists believe the loess deposits in the southern part of Europe's Great Lowland may have been blown there from huge fields of dried mud that were left after the glaciers of the Ice Age melted. See **Ice Age.**

lyric poet. A poet who writes short poems that express personal emotions, such as love, sorrow, or patriotism.

Mann (man), **Thomas,** 1875-1955. A famous German novelist of the twentieth century, born in Lübeck. Thomas Mann opposed Nazism, and left Germany in 1933. He was a professor at Princeton University for a time, then moved to California. Later he moved to Switzerland, where he lived until his death. Mann is noted for his philosophical

stories that deal with difficult human problems.

Marx (märks), **Karl,** 1818-1883. A German philosopher and radical reformer whose theories form the main foundations of modern socialism and communism. Born in Trier, the son of a lawyer, Marx studied law and philosophy. He became a socialist, and worked out an economic theory of history according to which the final triumph of the working class was inevitable.

Marxism-Leninism. The theory and practice of communism as developed by Lenin, the leader of the Russian Revolution of 1917. Lenin based his ideas on the thinking of the German philosopher Karl Marx. Marxism-Leninism, as interpreted by Communist leaders, forms the basis of action for Communist parties throughout the world. See **communism.**

medieval (mē'di ē' vəl). Refers to the Middle Ages. See **Middle Ages.**

Mein Kampf (mīn kämpf'). A book by Adolf Hitler, in which he states his political beliefs and his thoughts on race. *Mein Kampf* ("My Struggle") became the "bible" of Nazis in Germany while Hitler was in power.

Mendelssohn (men'dəl sən), **Felix,** 1809-1847. A German musician and composer who was born in Hamburg. In 1835 he became director of concerts at Leipzig, and in 1841 was called to Berlin by the King of Prussia to become general music director of the Academy of Arts. Among his compositions are symphonies, concertos, and choral and chamber music.

Mercator (mèr kā'tər) **projection.** One of many possible arrangements of meridians and parallels on which a map of the world may be drawn. Devised by Gerhardus Mercator, a Flemish geographer who lived from 1512 to 1594. On a Mercator map, all meridians are drawn straight up and down, with north at the top. The parallels are drawn straight across, but increasingly farther apart toward the poles.

Middle Ages. The period of European history between ancient times, which ended with the fall of the Western Roman Empire, and modern times. The transition from the Middle Ages to modern times was gradual. Changes, however, took place more rapidly in some areas than in others. Western Europe had generally emerged into modern times by the end of the fifteenth century.

moor. Area of open rolling wasteland, usually somewhat marshy.

NATO. The North Atlantic Treaty Organization, an alliance formed in 1949 by the United States, Canada, and ten European nations for the purpose of defense against possible attack by the Soviet Union. Greece, Turkey, and West Germany were later admitted as members.

Nazi (nä′tsi) **Party.** The political party that controlled Germany from 1933 to 1945. It began after World War I as a small political organization, called the German Workers' Party. Shortly after it was founded, Adolf Hitler became a member, and in 1921 he became its undisputed leader. Hitler and his associates renamed the party the National Socialist German Workers' Party. The name "Nazi" came from the first two syllables of the German word for "national-socialist." The ideology of the Nazi Party emphasized aggressive nationalism and belief in "racial purity."

Nietzsche (nē′chə), **Friedrich Wilhelm,** 1844-1900. A German philosopher, born near Lützen in central Germany.

Nobel prizes. Prizes awarded for exceptional accomplishment in literature, science, or the promotion of international peace. Alfred Nobel, a Swedish inventor and manufacturer, left his wealth to establish these prizes, several of which usually are awarded each year. Nobel prizes have been awarded since 1901 by organizations in Sweden and Norway.

parallel (par′ə lel). An imaginary circle drawn east and west around the earth, parallel to the equator.

propaganda. Information prepared mainly to persuade people to believe or act in a certain way. (See page 180.)

reactionaries. Persons who favor a return to earlier political, economic, or social policies or conditions.

reparations. Usually, money, materials, or equipment paid by a defeated nation to a victorious nation to compensate for the war costs of the victor. This term also may be applied to payments made to nations or individuals to compensate for injustices or the property losses of individuals. For example, West Germany made payments to Israel for crimes against the Jews under the Hitler regime, and Israel paid Arab refugees for their property losses during the war between Israel and several Arab states that was fought in 1948.

Saar (sär). A heavily industrialized region in western Germany, bordering on France and Luxembourg, that is also important for its deposits of coal. From 1920 to 1935 the Saar was under the control of the League of Nations. In 1935 the people of this region voted to rejoin Germany. After World War II the Saar was occupied by France. In 1957 the Saar again became a part of Germany.

Scandinavian peninsula. The long, narrow tongue of land in northern Europe

PRONUNCIATION KEY: hat, āge, cãre, fär; let, ēqual, tèrm; it, īce; hot, ōpen, ôrder; oil, out; cup, pùt, rüle, ūse; child; long; thin; ᴛʜen; zh, measure; ə represents a in about, e in taken, i in pencil, o in lemon, u in circus. For the complete key, see page 185.

occupied by the countries of Norway and Sweden.

Schiller (shil′ər), **Johann Christoph Friedrich von,** 1759-1805. A German playwright, poet, philosopher, and historian. Among his most outstanding works is the play *William Tell.*

Schumann (shü′män), **Robert Alexander,** 1810-1856. A German composer, musical director, and critic who was born at Zwickau.

Slavs. A large group of people who speak languages that are somewhat similar. They are descendants of early people who were living near the western border of what is now the Soviet Union when Christ was born. Russians, Poles, and Bulgarians all belong to the Slavic group of people.

socialism. Any one of several political and economic theories that challenge the right of private property, and favor the idea of using property for the public welfare. See **communism.**

square inch. An area that is equal in size to the area of a square that measures one inch on each side.

standard of living. The conditions that a person or group considers necessary in order to live properly. Among the factors considered in determining a standard of living are living conditions, working conditions, and the amount and kind of possessions of the person or group.

storm troopers. In Nazi Germany, politico-military units, made up of Nazi Party members whose main function was to break up meetings and perform other acts of violence in order to terrorize those who opposed Hitler.

subsidized farming. Farming that is assisted by government aid.

subsidy. Money or some other form of aid given by a government to a person or company as encouragement for continuing a useful activity.

tariffs. Duties, or taxes, that must be paid on articles brought into or taken out of a country.

technology. The name given to the entire body of knowledge, tools, machines, and other equipment with which man meets his needs.

values. Ideas or standards that a person considers to be worthwhile. A person's values influence the way he behaves. For instance, a person who believes that every individual is important will treat everyone he meets with consideration.

Wagner (väg′nər), **Wilhelm Richard,** 1813-1883. A German composer, writer, and musical director who was born at Leipzig.

Western. Refers to the civilization that developed, under the influence of Christianity, from the ideas of the ancient Greeks and Romans. In the last two centuries, Western civilization has been greatly influenced by the Industrial Revolution, which introduced power-driven machinery for the production of most goods.

World War I, 1914-1918. The first war in history that involved nearly every part of the world. The Central Powers — Germany, Austria, Turkey, and Bulgaria — were defeated by the Allies. These included Great Britain, France, Russia, Japan, and the United States.

World War II, 1939-1945. The second war in history that involved nearly every part of the world. The Allies, which included France, the United States, the United Kingdom, the Soviet Union, and many other countries, defeated the Axis. The Axis included mainly Germany, Italy, and Japan.

Zollverein (tsôl′fer īn′). A German customs union that was established by 1834. All restrictions on trade between the member states were abolished, and the tariffs on imports from other areas or foreign countries were low. The Zollverein did much to promote the economic growth of Germany.

INDEX

Explanation of abbreviations used in this Index:

p — pictures   *m* — maps

PRONUNCIATION KEY: h**a**t, **ā**ge, c**ā**re, f**ä**r; l**e**t, **ē**qual, t**ė**rm; **i**t, **ī**ce; h**o**t, **ō**pen, **ô**rder; **oi**l, **ou**t; c**u**p, p**ù**t; r**ü**le, **ū**se; **ch**ild; lo**ng**; **th**in; **ᴛн**en; **zh**, measure; **ə** represents **a** in about, **e** in taken, **i** in pencil, **o** in lemon, **u** in circus. For the complete key, see page 185.

PRONUNCIATION KEY: hat, āge, cãre, fär; let, ēqual, tėrm; it, īce; hot, ōpen, ôrder; oil, out; cup, pùt, rüle, ūse; child; long; thin; ᴛʜen; zh, measure; ə represents a in about, e in taken, i in pencil, o in lemon, u in circus. For the complete key, see page 185.

rivers and canals, 21-22, 24-25, 105, 118-121; *p* 118, 119; *m* 120
roads, *see* transportation
Roentgen (rent′gən), Wilhelm, 154-155, 156; *p* 155
Roman Catholic Church, 41-42, 43-44, 134, 135
Roman Empire, 37-38, 136; *m* 38
Rostock (räs′täk), East Germany, 121; *m* 140
Ruhr industrial area, 22, 93-94, 99, 103, 119, 120; *p* 22; *m* 95

Saar (sär), 103-104, 191; *p* 91, 110
Schiller (shil′ər), Friedrich von, 159, 192
schools, *see* education
Schumann (shü′män), Robert Alexander, 144, 161, 192
scientists, 154-157; *p* 154, 155, 157
SED, *see* Socialist Unity Party
skiing, 165; *p* 165
Slavs, 42, 192
soccer, 164; *p* 164
Socialist Unity Party, 88, 89, 90; *p* 35
Soviet (sō′vi et) Union, 14-15, 59-60, 61, 62, 76, 88, 99-101
sports and recreation, 163-168; *p* 163-168
standard of living, 135, 137, 192
steel, *see* industry, iron and steel

tariffs, 94, 96, 98, 192
temperature, *see* climate
textiles, *see* industry
theater, 165-166; *p* 166
Thirty Years' War, 45, 46

Tiergarten (tir′gärtən), 72, 78-79; *p* 78; *m* 72
time line, *see* history
trade, 98, 121, 128
trade fairs, 144-145; *p* 144
trade winds, 31, 32, 33; *m* 30, 31; *chart* 30
transportation, 122-125, 127-128; *p* 122-124, 127, 128; *m* 120, 125
    air, 122, 124-125; *p* 124; *m* 125
    East Germany, 125, 127-128; *p* 127
    railroads, 122, 123-124, 125; *p* 123, 156
    restrictions, 127-128; *p* 59, 128
    roads, 122, 124, 125, 127; *p* 122, 127, 128
    water, 93, 94, 118-120, 121, 122, 123, 125, 127; *p* 93, 118, 119; *m* 120
    West Germany, 122-125, 127; *p* 122-124
Treaty of Versailles (vär sī′), 56
Treaty of Westphalia, 45, 46
tuberculosis, 155

Ulbricht (ül′briHt), Walter, 90; *p* 63, 88
universities, *see* education, higher
Unter den Linden, 73, 80; *p* 79; *m* 72

Versailles, Treaty of, *see* Treaty of Versailles
Voice of America, 126
Volkskammer (fôlks′kä′mər), 89; *p* 89
Von Braun (vän broun′), Wernher, *p* 157

Wagner, Wilhelm Richard, 161, 192

Warsaw Pact, 61
waterpower, 25, 105
waterways, *see* rivers and canals
Weavers, The, 159
Weser (vā′zər) River, 22, 120; *p* 118; *m* 120
West Berlin, *see* Berlin
westerly winds, 27, 30, 31-32, 33; *m* 30, 31; *chart* 30
Western powers, 59, 60-61, 74, 76, 77
West Germany,
    area, 19
    capital, 86; *m* 86
    cities, 119, 120-121, 142-144; *p* 129, 130, 142; *m* 18, 140
    communication, 125, 126
    courts, 85
    education, 150-152; *p* 146, 150-152
    farming, 111-115; *p* 110-113, 115
    government, 61, 82-85, 87; *p* 35, 60, 81, 82, 84
    industry, 93, 97, 99, 106-108; *p* 91-93, 97, 106
    population, 130
    religion, 134, 135
    sports and recreation, 164-167; *p* 163-166
    standard of living, 135
    transportation, 122-125, 127; *p* 122-124
Westphalia, Treaty of, *see* Treaty of Westphalia
William Tell, 159
wind patterns, *see* climate
wood carving, 108; *p* 108
World War I, *see* history
World War II, *see* history
writers, 158-160, 161-162; *p* 159

X ray, 155; *p* 154

Zollverein (tsôl′fer īn′), 96, 192

PRONUNCIATION KEY: hat, āge, cãre, fär; let, ēqual, tèrm; it, īce; hot, ōpen, ôrder; oil, out; cup, pùt, rüle, ūse; child; long; thin; ᴛʜen; zh, measure; ə represents a in about, e in taken, i in pencil, o in lemon, u in circus. For the complete key, see page 185.